COMPASSIONATE CONSERVATISM BY DUMMYS

(The Wit and Wisdom of George W. Bush)

By Marley Roberts

Foreword by Warren Hinckle

Last Gasp
of San Francisco

Last Gasp of San Francisco
777 Florida Street
San Francisco, CA 94110
www.lastgasp.com

ISBN 0-86719-502-9 $14.95
additional copies $20.- postpaid to our address, or order
online at www.lastgasp.com.

Printed in Hong Kong

CONTENTS

INTRODUCTION:
The Family Business

By Warren Hinckle

Amerrica once had scabrous, wonderfully gross politicians, dingleberries and all, the best without compeer being Lyndon Johnson who had an adult toilet training complex. Johnson grew accustomed to taking his Lincoln Continental way out on the range on his Pedernales ranch when he had to do Number Two. A Secret Service agent was standing by the Connie Door to protect the Presidential modesty from passing jack rabbits when he felt a warming sensation down his pants leg. The President had returned from doing his dooty in the bushes and was further relieving himself on the Grade 12 civil servant. "Mr. President," George V. Higgins quotes the man, whom he identified as one Henderson, "You're pissing on my leg." The President replied: "Henderson, Ah know I am. That's mah prerogative."

Johnson was fond of sitting on the Oval Office crapper while discussing economic policy with his blueblood secretary of the treasury Douglas Dillon as the man twisted with patrician embarrassment. Tom Wicker once told me a best-of-LBJ story about receiving a command invitation to the Pedernales ranch at the time Wicker in his column in the *New York Times* was lambasting Johnson's Ahab-like pursuit of the Vietnam War. When Wicker arrived at the ranch he was graciously received and told he would get a call from the President in the morning. The phone rang at 5 a.m. Wicker was asked to meet the President downstairs in a half hour. Johnson said, "Let's take a ride, Tom." The president piled into the front seat of the Lincoln alongside his Secret Service driver and the columnist sat alone in the back seat as the Continental bounced along at 80 mph past brush and tumbleweed. The President didn't say word one to him.

At last Johnson signaled the driver to stop. His first spoken words of the morning to Wicker were, "The President has to take a shit." Johnson got unceremoniously out of the car and headed for a clump of bushes. Shortly thereafter he reappeared from the bushes and said to the Secret Serviceman, "The President has no paper. Yah all have any paper there?"

"Only the *New York Times*," said the driver.

"That'll do just fine," Johnson said. He headed back into the brush newspaper in hand. He returned after several minutes and got back into the front seat of the Lincoln which raced off across the prairie at high speed. Johnson didn't say another word to the columnist in the back seat until they reached the ranch house and got out of the car.

1

The Family Business

The president shook the *Times*man's hand and said, "I want to thank you, Tom, for the use of your newspaper."

I relate these crypto-scatological LBJ tales to remind the reader that, love them or leave them, there were once in this country politicians who were real people -- loons, crooks, serial adulterers, all the things that real people are -- running for, and sitting in, the Oval Office. But in the first presidential race of the new century we are saddled with two dweebs from wealthy, powerful political families who in their wibbledy, wobbledy strivings for perfection have achieved the apotheosis of un-interestingness.

Though both Gore and Bush are iodine-deficient in the salt of character there is a difference between the two Old Maids. The difference is family. Al Gore's father was a Senator before him and all that good stuff. However the Bush family is a horse of another color. The family business of the Bush dynasty is politics -- defined as money, the oil business, the spy business and its interconnections with Ivy League law firms and banking houses. Bill Kristol in the Murdoch-right *Weekly Standard* said the "Bush network (in the Republican Party) *is* the Establishment." Howard Fineman in the lib-chic *New Yorker* called the Bushes "the WASP Corleones." The truth is that both statements are true.

George W. Bush Jr. as the beneficiary of the family business never had to study hard or work a day in his life to get rich or get ahead in politics. The family connections took care of everything. All was handed to him, as we shall see. He worked at nothing. He earned nothing by himself, yet he got rich. George W. Bush *fils* was financially coddled by friends of his father who poured an amazing amount of money into Junior's losing oil ventures during the time George Bush Sr. was first running for the Republican presidential nomination in 1980, then sitting at the right hand of Ronald Reagan as his vice president and the presumptive heir to the Republican Party's control of the White House. And things got even better when his father was president.

George Jr., sometimes called Shrub, depending on your penchant for cute little nicknames -- "'Shrub ,' a play on the Spanish word for bush, as in plant, was coined by former Texas Governor Ann Richards of acidic tongue, whom Bush defeated for re-election (in a address to the Democratic Convention in 1988 Richards said Shrub's father was born with a silver foot in his mouth) -- returned these financial favors by doing everything he could, as Governor of Texas, for the rich people who helped him on the way up. To Junior making nice to corporate America is a obligation of class. Now he is carrying the Republican flag for the presidency. And he thinks Greeks are 'Grecians.'

The Family Business

You've got to know the territory, Professor Harold Hill sings in *The Music Man*. It is difficult and can be frustrating to attempt to understand George W. Bush Jr. -- there's not much there, there, as Gertrude Stein said of Oakland before Jerry Brown -- without knowing where he came from, which was not Texas, but from a family which fairly perfected the profitable symbiosis of government and business.

It is an axiom of the Republican Establishment embodied in the Bushes that winning is easier with the right connections. Shrub Bush didn't have to work hard to succeed because he knew people. People who knew people. The people who helped Junior get ahead in business and in politics were within six degrees of separation of the oil industry, the banking establishment, the legal seraphim --- and the intelligence community. They were linked in an Old Boy network by the process whereby the intelligence world used the commercial world to cover its misdeeds -- and did commercial favors in return.

The mutual backscratching of people who know people who are close to the "clandestine services of the United States" (a phrase of art coined by Watergate's E. Howard Hunt) is the formula for the success of the entire Bush political family -- beginning with Old Wiffenpoof himself, former Connecticut Senator Prescott Bush Sr., Yalie father to former CIA Director and former veep Yalie President George W. Bush, and grandfather to three politicized grandsons all of whom did well in the Family Business: young Neil, the bad-boy entrepreneur whom the U.S. government had to bail out of a Colorado Savings and Loan disaster with the standard vague mob and CIA connections, Governor Jeb Bush of Florida who was the family's liaison with the CIA-spawned anti-Castro Cuban right and its sometimes shadowy mob and intelligence connections and was in the penumbra of shadowy Florida Savings and Loans deals (as vice president George Bush Sr. intervened to slow federal regulation of a Florida S & L that later was revealed to have been looted by people with Mafia and CIA affiliations,) and of course there's George W. Junior who became a millionaire through connections.

(Even when George Junior appeared to find financial friends on his own they had the familiar DNA of CIA-cum oil-cum mysterious Cayman Island corporations-cum shady intelligence operations- background. An early investor in one of Junior's oil and gas operations was Jim Bath, who Junior said he became friends with in the Texas Air National Guard and considered "a lot of fun." After his tour of duty with the Air National Guard Bath went into the airline business in Texas where he was peripherally involved in the illegal Contra supply operation which was overseen from the office of then Vice President George W. Bush. Bath thereafter became the financial advisor to several Saudi Arabian Sheiks who were in turn connected to the notorious Bank of Credit and Commerce International (BCCI) which was Oliver North's bank of choice for disguising money going to arm the Contras and the bank traditionally used by the CIA for funding covert operations. A former partner of Bath testified in a Houston lawsuit that Bath told him he had been personally recruited into the CIA in 1976 by then-CIA Director George Bush. In 1990 the *Houston Post* reported that the Department of Defense was paying millions of dollars more than necessary -- some $12 million -- to buy aviation fuel from Bath's company at Ellington Field, where Bath had a sweetheart $650 a month lease.)

Many of the Bush-noir stories in this introduction come from more than a decade of digging into the several generations of the Bush family. This biographical excavation began in 1988 when Bush Sr. was running for president and Emile de Antonio, the master left wing documentary filmmaker of *Point of Order*, *Millhouse* and other classics of the genre, was considering making movie about the Bush clan. Dee and I had been friends since the time I edited *Ramparts* magazine during its muckraking years of the late 60s and Dee and I discovered that we shared a disdain for some of the orthodoxies and style of the left.

I was writing a series of columns for the *San Francisco Examiner* called "Bush and The Drug Wars" which detailed the vice president's abject failure as the Reagan administration's Anti Drug Czar and his chattel relationship with the intelligence-industrial complex. Dee and I had been talking about doing a project together and over a few drinks settled on the idea of launching a magazine to be called *Smoking Gun* which would provide the raw stuff for de Antonio's movie by exploring the intercises between the world of spooks and the world of business with particular emphasis on the Bush clan as the paradigm for profit. Both of us had sources among disaffected members of the intelligence community and some of *Ramparts* former tenacious New Left researchers contributed to the project and deAntonio utilized his contacts among the East Coast financial Brahmin. In short time we discovered a bizarre network of anti-Bush researchers from underground press-niks to frustrated upperclass suburban housewives bent on lying bare the sins of the Bush fathers and the Bush sons.

The *Smoking Gun* project stopped with de Antonio's untimely death in 1991. Some of this research was utilized in the 1993 book *Deadly Secrets* which I co-authored with ex-FBI agent William Turner (which was a revised version updated through the Bush presidency of our 1981 book *The Fish Is Red* which chronicled three decades of the U.S. secret war against Cuba.) The Bush-noir research continued sporadically thereafter as the score of file boxes secreted in my basement will attest. The view afforded from those boxes of the Bush family and of what George

W. Bush Jr. is really all about is not reflected in the books that have been published about Bush during this campaign year and the reader may find the following brief overview of the Bush family, grandfather, father and sons, instructive.

The oil business and the intelligence business have historically been as close as the stamp to the envelope and grandfather Bush was there helping provide the glue. Yale was the preferred agent of delivery. Yale is America's senior school for spies, a checkered history deliciously detailed in the book *Cloak and Gown* at Yale. A statue of Nathan Hale, America's first spy, is prominent on campus and the Yale alumni ranks are diamond-studded with Ivy League CIA agents.. (The CIA was doing the bidding of the American oil companies even before the landmark year of 1953, when CIA operative Kermit Roosevelt--grandson of Teddy and cousin to FDR--was dispatched to Iran by Secretary of State John Foster Dulles and his CIA-director brother Allen Dulles to get rid of "That madman Mosadegh." In retrospect the coup was unfortunate for American foreign policy since the reinstated Shah was eventually tossed out, and the Ayatollah and the mullahs took charge of Iran's oil.)

Please welcome the late Prescott Bush, former Republican senator from Connecticut. At Yale he was a great golfer and a Wiffenpoofer who sang a mean harmony. His cause was Skull and Bones, the secret Yale society with twisted roots back in sixteenth-century Bavaria. The impish young Prescott and another Skull and Bones joker ventured on a dare to steal Geronimo's skull from his grave in Fort Sill, Oklahoma. They fled with the skull back to the Skull and Bones crypt on the Yale campus and hid it like a dog would a bone. The Apaches were understandably perturbed. Some decades later, representatives of the tribe came to Yale to try to get their main man's skull back, but the Apaches said that the Bonesmen tried to palm someone else's skull off of them.

Young George Sr. joined his father's secret society in 1948 and performed the Skull and Bones initiation rites such as laying in a coffin or the next best thing and recounting your sexual history to the group. (Bonesmen have few secrets from each other, but have few qualms about lying to the rest of the world.) George W. Bush Sr. matured in a moral atmosphere where lying became an art form. He had lots of practice. As Director of the Central Intelligence Agency, where prevarication is a competitive lifestyle, he stonewalled the Justice Department to protect his predecessor as CIA director, Richard Helms, and in doing so protected, for a time, the CIA's dirty secrets--its care and feeding of domestic terrorists, the agency's splitting the sheets with the Mafia in attempts to assassinate President Fidel Castro, and our intelligence services long relationship with organized crime and drug traffickers.

(Historical note: This untoward alliance originated during World War

Deuce when the CIA's predecessor, the Office of Strategic Services (OSS), and its sister spook agency, the Office of Naval Intelligence, cut deals with the Mafia to keep peace on the New York waterfront in return for most favored nation status for Lucky Luciano, and entered into indiscreet relationships with Chaing-Kai-shek's opium-smuggling secret police. In the postwar years the fledgling spy agency enlisted as Cold War "assets" the heroin-smuggling Corsican network and earned the further goodwill of the Sicilian Mafia. During the Vietnam War years the CIA joint-ventured with members of Southeast Asia's Golden Triangle; stories of the CIA's Air America cargo planes taking dope to market are legend. By the 70s the CIA was knee-deep in various operational levels of heroin, opium, marijuana and cocaine smuggling.)

As Vice President of the United States under the somnolent Reagan, Bush helped arm the Contras as a time when that was against the law--and he lied like a rug about it. By the time he became President in his own right in 1989, George Bush Sr. was, without compare the most professional liar in American politics.

Participation in the "clandestine services" is part of the Bush family tradition. Prescott Bush, Sr. served in Army intelligence during World War I. Jump to 1962, when Prescott Sr. and his good friend William J. Casey, an old hand from the OSS who later was Ronald Reagan's CIA director during the Iran-Contra scandal, set up the National Strategic Information Center, a right-wing think tank which, during the Reagen-Bush administration, pushed for increased covert operations. Prescott Jr., George Bush's older brother, was a prominent member of the Americares Foundation, which along with doing good deeds was linked to efforts to aid far-right elements in Honduras and Guatemala.

George W. Bush Sr.'s Skull and Bones networking and his family's intelligence connections have materially shaped his life, as they would come to effect the career of his son George Jr. The senior Bush was husbanded into the oil business at a tender age by Henry Neil Mallon, an old family friend and Skull and Bonesman. Mallon was also a close friend of America's Spook-in-Chief, Allen Dulles, and was especially helpful to Dulles in recruiting people into the CIA, according to a letter from Senator Prescott Bush to the Eisenhower White House. When Henry Neil Mallon died at a ripe old age in 1983, vice president Bush told the Associated Press: "He gave me my first real job and, when I started my first business, he was at my side... One of our sons, Neil Mallon Bush, was named for this wonderful man." Whether Mallon also recruited Bush into the CIA remains unknown, although Bush obliquely hinted at his prior connections with the agency in his 1988 campaign autobiography, *Looking Forward.* Bush wrote coyly that when

President Gerald Ford appointed him CIA director in 1976. "I'd come to the CIA with some general knowledge of how it operated."

The senior Bush's first known cozy-up with the CIA was in the late 1950s when he was making money in offshore oil drilling in the Caribbean. Castro's 1959 revolution could hardly have been more welcome to the free booting oil fraternity as it was to the Mafia. At the time of the Bay of Pigs invasion in 1961, Bush had his rigs strategically positioned thirty miles north of Cuba near Cay Sal -- an island exclusively used by the CIA as a service station for covert operations.

George W. Bush Sr. hid some family secrets when he ran for president in 1988. One was the relationship between himself and Jorge Diaz Serrano, who had been convicted of looting Mexico's national oil monopoly Pemex. After learning the oil business from the ground up -- with the special assistance of CIA recruiter Mallon -- Bush formed his own oil company, Zapata Petroleum Corporation, in 1953. He raised eyebrows throughout the Texas oil industry when he established an unusual relationship with Mexican oilman Serrano. In 1960, Bush and Diaz Serrano entered into a joint venture in a Mexican drilling company called Permargo. (Bush's 50 percent interest in the corporation was hidden because his ownership violated Mexican law. Permargo received government favors as a Mexican-owned company, but only 100 percent Mexican-owned companies could receive such special consideration.)

Permargo had lucrative contracts with Pemex and in 1975 Diaz Serrano became head of Pemex, a position he held for five years. Shortly after Bush's ex-partner took charge of Pemex, agency sources say the CIA began using Pemex as a cover for secret ops. This was when Bush was CIA director in 1976. Reports thereafter surfaced of Pemex's being bilked of millions during Serrano's tenure and in 1983 Bush's former partner was convicted of defrauding the Mexican government and was sentenced to five years in prison.

When *Barron's* financial magazine looked into Bush's shadowy Mexican operation, investigative reporter Jonathan Kwitny found that the key Zapata records detailing Bush's business relationship with J Diaz Serrano had disappeared from the Securities and Exchange Commission files. They had been "inadvertently destroyed." a few months after Bush was sworn in as Vice President, the SEC said.

If the young George Bush Sr. was not a CIA "asset," he was certainly user-friendly to the agency. He could not have been anything else considering that his family brought him up to revere spooks, and from a tender age he kept their company. Two of his tap mates in the Skull and Bones went on to become top CIA operatives in the 1950's. Another fraternity-mate, William F. Buckley, Jr., was assigned to the CIA station in Mexico City in the 1950's when E. Howard Hunt was in charge. George Bush's 1980 grab for the presidential gold ring was supported by a virtual army of spies. Retired CIA agents came out of the shadows to do precinct work. *The Washington Post* reported in 1988 that "no presidential campaign in recent memory--perhaps--has attracted as much support from the intelligence community as the campaign of former CIA director George Bush".

During his failed 1988 attempt to wrestle the Republican nomination from Ronald Reagan, Bush received campaign contributions from Skull and Bones members with go-go messages written on the checks in the Yale society's secret code. In 1981, when Bush and his wife, Barbara, hosted a reunion of his Skull and Bones class at the vice presidential mansion in the federal city, twelve aging Bonesmen and their spouses attended (a group photo published in the *Washington Post* memorialized the occasion.) When Bush had to console himself with the second spot on the ticket--his selection as Veep was engineered by his father's friend, Reagan's all-knowing campaign manager, William Casey--Bush's spook supporters moved en masse into the Reagan-Bush campaign where they became busy little bees destabilizing President Jimmy Carter's re-election campaign. They managed to lift Carter's briefing book for his television debate with Bush, allowing Bush to more easily bushwhack Carter, set up Carter's feckless brother Billy to look like a cheerleader for Libya and planted moles in the National Security Council and the White House situation room to keep track of Carter's every move during the Iranian hostage crisis.

The intelligence community had reason to go all the way for Shrub's father: He had gone all the way for them. In 1976 when he was DCI--CIA shorthand for Director of Central Intelligence -- Bush burned bridges to keep President Gerald Ford's barking dogs from former DCI Richard Helms, who was being hounded by the Justice Department for lying to Congress. Helms had been running what LBJ had called "a damned Murder Inc. in the Caribbean" which he of course lied about to Congress -- along with the lying about the plot to kidnap General Schneider of Chile (which resulted in his death) and the other dirty little arrangements that resulted in the murder of Chilean President Salvador Allende and the installation of a military dictatorship. Bush stonewalled Ford's Justice Department to protect Helms but a year later Helms pleaded no contest to two criminal counts of failing to testify "fully, completely and accurately" before Congress. Helms was so distressed by what he considered infidel attempts to pry into the agency's secrets--the company's "family jewels"--that he accosted CIA critic Daniel Schorr, then a correspondent for CBS, in a Capitol Hill hallway and called him a "cocksucker" loud enough for all within the Beltway to hear.

DCI Bush saved some seventy current and former CIA agents from the dock by simply refusing to turn the requisite CIA records over to the Justice Department, which was seeking to prosecute the spies. In the course of his defense Bush did not raise the issue of the national interest (as past CIA directors had in similar circumstances) or the Nixonian concept of national security. Instead he took the resolutely stubborn position that because the CIA had told its operatives to do what they had done, it could not be a crime.

Among the secrets Bush protected from public exposure and prosecution was the CIA's infiltration of the Drug Enforcement Agency (DEA) shortly after it was formed out of the old Bureau of Narcotics and Dangerous Drugs in 1973. The CIA used the DEA as deep cover for dozens of its anti-Castro Cuban contract agents who were profitably involved in drug smuggling while they did the Lord's work for the CIA; if caught, they received immunity from prosecution because of their protected status as CIA "assets."

Congress had formally banned U.S. help to the terrorist Contras warring against the leftist Sandinista government in Nicaguara. But groups within the CIA and the ever-eager Lt. Col. Ollie North figured a way around the prohibition -- while the Beltway media, late to the story, never twigged to the fact that the forbidden contra-resupp'y op was largely coordinated from vice president Bush's office by former CIA types on his staff. When CIA-connected narcotraffickers involved in the Contra-resupply ran afoul of federal prosecutors they were protected from prosecution to the extent that two career U.S. attorneys in Miami, R. Jerome Stanford and Richard Gregorie, resigned in frustration. Gregorie testified before a Senate committee that the CIA interference in drug prosecutions was a "constitutional crisis."

Although George W. Bush Jr. freely admits to binge drinking of the "3 B's" -- brandy, bourbon and B & B -- before he experienced a dry epiphany at 40, Shrub has been almost combative in his refusal to discuss -- affirm, or deny -- his use of cocaine in college and thereafter. The pregnant rumors of young Bush dealing coke at Yale continue to swell and Houston was awash in a social sea of inexpensive recreational cocaine in his post-college years. Ironic as it may be, the wide availability of cocaine in the years George W. Junior was growing up -- the persistent reports that he was arrested for cocaine possession in Texas in 1972 but ducked formal charges through a diversion program with the paperwork successfully deep-sixed have never been convincingly dispelled -- were directly related to his father's compromised policies as America's Drug Czar.

The Family Business

The world of drug smuggling and the world of intelligence and secret special operations were a perfect fit for the many uses of subterfuge and official deniability that both required. This made it the more inane when Richard Nixon made the CIA the chief drug intelligence agency in 1973 -- a folly stubbornly perpetuated by Bush throughout his disastrous years as the Reagan administration's Drug Czar. He continued to assign the CIA to the War on Drugs and the CIA continued to undermine that war with the CIA exemption for its favored traffickers. During Bush's years minding the nation's drug store from 1981 to 1988 the metric tonnage of cocaine coming into the United States tripled, the price of coke fell more than 50 percent from what it had been at the beginning of the decade, and the crack war exploded in the inner cities of America with the CIA shepherding some of the suppliers.

UC Berkeley professor Peter Dale Scott, an expert on the connection between intelligence agencies and narcotraffickers, summed up the senior Bush's contribution to his son's illicit recreational habits thus succinctly: "When the U.S. was involved in covert operations in Southeast Asia in the 1960s and 1970s, we had a heroin epidemic on this continent. In the 1980s, when some of the same people were involved in a covert operation in Central America, we had a cocaine epidemic. That's not a coincidence."

This CIA-immunity continued throughout the 80s when CIA-connected narcotraffickers contributed to the illegal resupply of the Contras by turning over part of the profits of their CIA-protected drug smuggling -- a fact of more than historical interest because the rising financial fortunes of the senior Bush's sons have been in one manner or the other connected with many of the financial institutions or individuals involved in secreting the Contra funding, such as the aforementioned mob and CIA-connected Bank of Credit and Commerce International (BCCI.) This included as we shall soon see George W. Bush Jr.'s 1990' financial windfall from the Harken Energy Corporation, a mysterious Texas oil company that the Wall Street Journal reported had a "mosaic of BCCI connections."

Just as George W. Bush Jr. took on governmental service as sort of a family and class obligation rather from than any deep-rooted beliefs other than to follow the money, his other political brother, Jeb, now Governor of Florida, followed the inevitably twisted paths of the Family Business on a road to wealth shaded with the cumulus clouds of political scandal. One example from Jeb Bush's career is illustrative of just how much the Family Business methods have effected the careers of all of the Bush sons.

In the mid-1980's, the bilingual Jeb Bush became the Republican Party's unofficial ambassador to Miami's Cuban-American community; he also served as an enabler and cheerleader for Miguel Recarey, Jr., a rich anti-Castro Cuban with connections, both peripheral and mainline, to organized crime who also ran a mysterious "debt collection" business, rumored to be under contract to an intelligence agency, which employed two dozen secretaries to transcribe bugged telephone conversations.

An exile to Miami from a wealthy pre-Castro Havana family whose his uncle had been the dictator Fulgencio Batista's minister of health, Recarey artfully traded on his anti-Castro credentials to build a mammoth health maintenance organization, International Medical Centers (IMC), and in a short time had become the medical-care czar of Dade County. Recarey openly bragged on his close connections with Florida mob boss Santos Trafficante (an early recruit to the CIA's assassination attempts against Castro) and the mob boss provided short term financing for Recarey's HMO. "As far back as the 1960's he (Recarey) had ties with reputed racketeers who had operated out of pre-Castro Cuba and who later forged an anti-Castro alliance with the CIA," *The Wall Street Journal* reported in 1988.)

Recarey got a jump start in the HMO business by signing up 10,000 Cuban political prisoners and their families as they stepped off the plane in Miami after Castro released them from jail. A big time contributor to both the Democratic and Republican parties Recarey paid handsome fees to former Reagan - Bush campaign officials to represent him in Washington----$400,000 to the p.r. firm of Black, Manfor and Stone, and $300,000 to former Reagan campaign manager John Sears.

Notwithstanding this high-powered help, Recarey had to ask the Vice President's son to make a key phone call to the Department of Health and Human Services when he needed a waiver of Medicare rules to expand his heath empire. which was largely dependent on Medicare payments for the elderly. After Jeb Bush called a federal regulator in 1985 and (according to later testimony in Congress) said that "America could trust Mike Recarey," the federal overseers suspended the regulation that no more than 50 percent of an HMO's income could come from Medicare payments.

Despite the fact that, as a CPA, Recarey had been busted for failing to file income tax returns, and had a history of fraud allegations in previous business dealings with Florida hospitals, after Jeb Bush's glowing telephone call the federal hospital regulators further relaxed the rules for Recarey to the extent that income from Medicare checks grew to more than eighty percent of his HMO's receipts. At the time of its billion-dollar collapse in 1987, Recarey's HMO was the largest recipient of Medicare benefits in the nation and many thousands of elderly Floridians never received medical care because IMC had already spent their Medicare checks.

The man whom Jeb Bush certified as trustworthy was running a classic mob-style "bust-out" operation where bills weren't paid, services weren't provided, and much of its Medicare income of more than $30 million a month was siphoned off to Recarey's other business ventures. IMC had links to a private network that supported the Contras and federal investigators suspected that some of the hundreds of millions in Medicare funds that disappeared into the "black hole" of Recarey's accounting went to the Nicaraguan rebels. The construction supervisor at IMC was Jose Baulto, a Bay of Pigs veteran who in the early 1980s was an advisor to Argentine intelligence officers training torture squads in Central America. He later "coordinated" IMC free medical aid to the Contras. It was thereafter discovered that many wounded Contras were well enough to be actively involved in drug smuggling.)

Miguel Recarey's friends in high places such as Jeb Bush gave him a magic wand when it came to the government   Although he was under indictment for massive fraud and racketeering in the IMC collapse, Recarey was allowed to keep his passport, get passports for his children, sell off assets--including condos, Ferraries, and BMW's--and he received an "expedited" $2.2 million tax refund from the IRS, all before fleeing the country in 1988.

The *Miami Herald* reported that at the time Jeb Bush intervened with Washington on Recarey's behalf, Bush's Florida real estate firm stood to make $250,000 in a deal Bush was negotiating for IMC. Even though the deal did not materialize, Recarey in 1986 paid Bush Realty $75,000 for work on the project,.

The brainbox of the presidential Bush *fils* is the subject of this mind-reading (in his own words) volume. His is not a story of inventing yourself but of doing what he was told, and what was expected, and taking what was given him, which was quite a lot. Among the attributes he learned from his father was a penchant for secrecy or specific vagueness (the crude of tongue would simply call it the ability to lie like a rug) about certain aspects of his background and the coincidence of having key records lost.

Decades after the SEC lost the records of George W. Bush Sr.'s Mexican oil operation, George W. Bush Jr. became mired in a contretemps over his windfall sale of two-thirds of his stock in Harken Energy in June of 1990 which appeared to be a combination of the traditions of insider dealing and the rat-leaving-the-ship. Bush pocketed a plumb $318,430 profit on his shares at a time when the Harken board, of which Bush was a member, had been informed that the company was gliding toward the shoals of financial peril. And two months after Bush unloaded his stock Iraq invaded Kuwait and Harken's shares crashed precipitously leaving the other shareholders in the bathtub. Bush was in a position to have a manner of insider's knowledge of that further geopolitical threat to the firm as one of his fellow Harken board members, Talat Othman, had become a frequent visitor to the White House and was advising Junior's father on oil policy on the eve of President Bush's going to war for oil in the mideast.

There was no great publicity when the opportunistic George Junior dumped his Harken stock because he kept the dumping operation a secret. Securities and Exchange Commission regulations require that any insider such as Bush certainly was, report in a timely fashion, immediately is preferred, the sale of any large block of stock so as to alert the smellers of lesser-informed stockholders that an insider was making a move that might signal a precipitous change in the stock's value. Bush did not report the sale until a full eight months later, after the entire Gulf War during which Harken shares fall like a stone down a well had come and gone.

When Ann Richards of sharp memory and tongue raised the Great Stock Dump as a violation of SEC rules during her 1994 race against Bush for governor, Bush said matter of factly that he had too filed the proper papers with the SEC and the SEC must have misplaced them (as it lost his father's records.) This time, a SEC spokesperson did not fess up to any missing records but simply said that they had no record of the timely papers Bush insisted he had filed.

This was a very polite way of inferring that George W. Bush Jr. was carrying out the family tradition of lying -- lying about the whereabouts of Geronomino's skull, lying about narcotraffickers profiting through the illegal Contra resupply operation, lying about filing required disclosure papers with the SEC. A lie is a lie is lie, but the luck of the Family Business held steady and Shrub was not fined by the SEC.

The Harken Energy story is part of a mosaic -- along with Jeb Bush's involvement with the bust-out expert Recarey, and Neil Mallon Bush's role in the profitable-for-some S & L bailout in Colorado -- of the Bush Family Business and an m.o. for what a reasonable person would expect of a new Bush administration should George W. Bush Jr. succeed in riding a golden elephant into the Federal City.

Junior became a large shareholder in Harken because he sort of tumbled down the rabbit hole left by the previous bailouts of his earlier, failing oil companies. According to Bill Minutaglio adoring biography of Shrub, First Son, as Junior partied his way through Yale -- in case you just have to know he did not dance nude on top of a bar, it was just a toga with a very short hemline -- he groused continually about the then-60s aborning concept of affirmative action. He had no use for "guilt-ridden" students who worried about equal rights for blacks and opening windows of opportunity for the poor. Yet in making his way through the Texas oil sludge the Junior Bush had no qualms about accepting the country's oldest form of affirmative action -- the largess that accompanies a dynastic legacy.

Shrub's business ventures in the West Texas oil town of Midland -- where his oilman father first got his hands dirty -- hardly make him out to be the "bulldog on the pantleg of opportunity" as he once described himself. For his first go in 1978, after a failed, presumptuous run for Congress, he tied up some rights and began drilling -- but the only money that came in was some $2 million in investments from politically connected friends of his ex-CIA chief father. He walked away from that company with the investors gentlemanly writing off their losses which included more than three quarters of a million bucks of their money in Shrub's jeans.

At the same time he started another oil company, Arbusto Energy -- he claimed that Arbusto was the Spanish word for bush but as we know when Ann Richards looked up bush in a Spanish dictionary she found "shrub" -- and started lining up close to $5 million in investors, most of that coming from Bush family friends in Connecticut. By 1982 Arbusto was also going down the oil drilling equivalent of the tubes -- after almost $5 million in investments it had a book value of less than $400,000 -- when miraculously out of the wings came an investor from Panama, a friend of Shrub's now-vice president father and a college buddy of James Baker III (who would later become President Bush's secretary of state) who shelled out $1 million for ten percent of a failing company worth less than $400,000.

By 1984 Arbusto -- renamed Bush Exploration in a patent attempt to capitalize on the vice-presidential name -- was teetering again only to be rescued by an out-of-state oil company named Spectrum 7, which was owned by two friends of his father who were to become very substantial contributors to his father's 1998 presidential campaign. The reason given for saving Shrub's company was that Spectrum 7 needed his management expertise (mind, Shrub thus far in his oil career had exhibited expertise only in creating substantial tax loses for his wealthy investors) and what better way to get the man than to buy his company? George W. Bush Jr. thereby became the third largest shareholder in Spectrum 7. Shrub's oil bad luck held true to form and by 1999 Spectrum appeared headed for the oil round file. But by 1989 Shrub's father was president of the United States and Harken Energy Corporation dispelled the gloom of the horizon by materializing to acquire the stumbling Spectrum and George W. Bush Jr. along with it. Harken was run by a Republican fund raising honcho who had President Bush symps pouring in investments for a acquisition run of energy related companies which blessed-ly came to include the distressed property of the president's son.

One might say that all's well that ends well for affirmative action for the rich -- President Bush's two campaign contributors got their money back in spades with the Harken acquisition and Shrub landed upright with some half million in Harken stock and a fat annual six figure consulting fee -- but then Shrub apparently felt the unfamiliar need to work for his money and was instrumental in securing a $25 million funding for Harken Energy that was messy with many of the players in past Family Business dealings including but not limited to various oil Sheiks and CIA and mob-user friendly funding institutions, not the least of which was the notorious BCCI.

The fortunes of Harken -- which *Time* with its usual concern for under-statement described as one of the most "eccentric outfits ever to drill for oil" -- were on the rise because to the astonishment and envy of most everyone in the oil explo-ration business Harken secured an exclusive oil exploration contract with the tiny Persian Gulf emirate of Bahrain. This award was considered odd because Harken had no practical experience, zero, zilch in off shore exploration. But the unexpected news was so good that the Bass Brothers, those well known proponents of equal opportu-nity, and likewise huge contributors to President Bush's election campaign, popped up to take a piece of the Harken exploration action.

The enlightened self interest that is at bedrock of the Bush Family Business is evident in the most cursory examination of the good fortunes of George W. Bush Jr. and Harken Energy, stars shooting around the shoddy sun of the Bank of Credit and Commerce International (which has long since folded its tent and crept into the dark night of the history of international financial daring-do.) One of the unstated functions of BCCI, aside from being a cupboard for the CIA to hide its dirty dishes, was to funnel Mideast petroriches into forms of political influence in America. There is little question in the minds of most sophisticated observers that the thirty-five year oil exploration contract Harken so surprisingly snagged with the tiny emirate of Bahrain was to bring the blessings of Allah on President Bush's son. The oilman who brought the Bahrainis to Harken Energy had a long history with BCCI as an advisor to many of the Saudi royales who were among the bank principals.

And when Shrub went on his money raising raid for Harken where did he park his stetson but on the doorstep of the powerhouse investment bank Stephens Inc. of Little Rock -- whose boss' had been a substantial contributor to President Bush's successful 1988 presidential campaign and soon in the best traditions of Little Rock patriotism became an important backer of Bill Clinton's presidential tours of duty. To crank out Harken's $25 million offering, Stephens Inc. steered Shrub's people to a London subsidiary of the Union Bank of Switzerland, which was a joint venture partner with BCCI in a Geneva-based bank. Union Bank was involved in intriguing financial front page stories from the mysterious movement of quantities of Ferdinand Marcos' gold out of the Phillipines to the sexy Nugen Hand scandal over an obscure Australian bank that became famous when in imploded in the 1980s in a explosion of drug transactions, secret arms deals, covert intelligence and business operations that rewrote the limits of CIA-connected white collar fraud and chicanery (in yet another twist of synergy, the son of a Harken Energy board member was the lawyer for Nugen Hand's main man in the Phillipines.)

Shrub's other big financial killing -- his jackpot from his sale of his share in the Texas Rangers baseball team -- in which a $600,000 investment turned with Harry Potter-type magic into a $15 million profit, was a manifestly hypocritical perversion of George W. Bush Jr.'s off-stated anti-tax, less governmental-interference philosophy. The riches that the Rangers made came from no less than mau mauing the taxpayers by extorting the good citizens of Arlington. It became in the immortal words of Richard Nixon perfectly clear to the baseball loving Arlington electorate that the Rangers would pack up their bats and take a hike if the taxpayers didn't pick up all the costs of building a new stadium for the team -- along with ignoring Shrub's religious adoration of the rights of private property by using eminent domain powers to condemn private property for the good of Shrub's stadium. The fiscal hijacking that came darn near to doubling the book value of the team without Shrub having to endure the pain of opening his wallet. Shrub sold his 11 percent of the team with the socialized stadium in 1988 for more than $15 million. This time, the taxpayers did the scut work for him.

George W. Bush Jr.'s Texas is a state where living high on the hog is akin to godliness and the usual rules of probity don't apply. Part of Junior's unprecedented ability to raise absolutely scary amounts of money for his presidential bid was the fact that that Texas doesn't have the usual limits on campaign contributions from individuals, and by eschewing matching federal funding Shrub didn't have to abide by the federal limits on campaign contributions, either. The other part of Shrub's fund raising ability is from the financial overflow from grateful Texas tycoons who have benefited sinfully from Governor Bush's austerity budgets based on tax cuts for the rich and the back of his hand for the poor -- another manifest hypocrisy from the man who had the famous nerve to chide Washington Republicans that it was wrong to balance the federal check book "on the backs of the poor," which is exactly what he has done in Texas.

That Texas is so awash in easy political money for the right person is in no little way the residue of the rape and pillage of Texas Savings and Loans in the 80s where the plunder was so vast as to stagger the mind of a Roman emperor. The epicenter of the national S & L fiscal earthquake was in Texas and by the time the financial dead bodies in other states were added up you had the biggest rip off of the taxpayers in American history. The looting of the S & L by a combination of good 'ol boys and mob and CIA-connected operators was the equal of a mob bust-out operation where a company is built up and drained of its assets --sound familiarly like Jeb Bush's friend Recarey?-- and the boys then take a hike leaving the creditors holding the bag. Only in this case, the luckless creditors were the U.S. taxpayers.

The wholesale pillaging of the S & Ls sprung from the Reagan-Bush policy of deregulating the thrifts which was a blanket invitation to the dance for swindlers of every stripe. The point man in the Reagan-Bush team in charge of the nominal overseeing of deregulation was vice president Bush who chaired the Bush Task Group on Regulation of Financial Services. The senior Bush here performed as effectively as he did in his disastrous role of Drug Czar. The then-vice president's son Neil Bush resigned as a director of the financially troubled and rumored mob-linked Silverado Savings in Colorado a few days after his father was won the Republican nomination for president in 1988. (*The National Thrift News*, the only trade paper on top of the scandal, later reported that the young Bush's oil and gas company had a $1 million line of credit from another bank owned by a developer who had borrowed more than $40 million from the doomed Silverado under Bush's watch.)

George W. Bush Sr. was elected president in 1988 in large part because the fantastic S & L scandal never surfaced as a campaign issue. For that inter-party cooperation one has to thank presidential nominee Bush, who was not about to breath a word on the subject lest it sink his campaign, and the Democratic vice presidential candidate, Senator Lloyd Bentsen, who had similar Texas-type reasons for not focusing on a scandal that involved far too many prominent politically connected Texans, both Republican and Democrat. The meltdown of the S & Ls would have been a scandal staining both parties; and at the end of the day the corrupt bipartisanship that has so benefited the fortunes of the Bush Family Business once again kept the silence.

Nathan Miller in his history of corruption in American politics, *Stealing From America*, traces governmental ripoffs from the Founding Fathers to Teapot Dome under Harding and the S & L scandal under the Reagan-Bush administrations and concludes that while both Democratic and Republican administrations have had their crooks, Republican administrations have been on balance the more corrupt (Nixon's tenure was the first time both a president and a vice president were unmasked as crooked), presumably because of the influx of businessmen to Washington who are so accustomed to mixing politics with business. The exemplar of the breed was Simon Cameron, the grafter who bought his way into Abraham Lincoln's cabinet where he became Secretary of War and wove an extraordinary web of corruption and bribery that set back the Union Army materially and significantly prolonged the carnage.

The S & L Texas of President Bush and the Texas administration of his son Governor Bush where the road was prepared to privatize welfare for profit, air pollution controls and other environmental regulations were relaxed, and in general big-contributing corporations could prescribe the type of governmental regulation they preferred, would make fine additions to an updated version of Miller's book. With George W. Bush Jr. the way of doing politics is the Family Business way which is to follow the money. Shrub simply doesn't know any other way. This is a matter of family culture, not of political philosophy. It is not something he thought of because, as the direct quotations that follow in this volume make evident, the man doesn't think much, just as he doesn't read much (he once said his favorite childhood book was "The Willie Mayes Story," which, he later allowed, was a story that wasn't really a book.)

Early in the campaign when Bush's lack of gravitas was being questioned (Molly Ivins has rightly pointed out that is is rather silly to say George W. Bush Jr. "governed" Texas for two terms because under the Lone Star State's Constitution the powers of the governor are so pitifully weak as to be nonexistent and the political heavy lifting is traditionally done by others) Shrub Bush began lugging around a hefty tome on the life of Secretary of State Dean Acheson, the contents of which he seemed to absorb primarily through osmosis.

What you see with George W. Bush Jr. is not what you get. What you get is the Family Business. #

Warren Hinckle, the recipient of the Thomas Paine and H. L. Mencken Awards, was the editor of Ramparts *magazine during its muckraking years in the late 1960s. He was the co-editor with Sidney Zion of* Scanlan's, *the magazine Richard Nixon hated most, and editor of filmmaker Francis Coppola's experimental* City of San Francisco *weekly. He has been a columnist for the* San Francisco Chronicle *and columnist and associate editor of the* San Francisco Examiner. *He is the author or co-author of many books includ-*

ing the critically acclaimed autobiography If You Have A Lemon Make Lemonade, *and with William W. Turner,* Deadly Secrets. *He lives in New York City and San Francisco, where he is publisher of* The Argonaut. *He is working on a socio-political history of the Bush family.*

FURTHER READING:

On George W. Bush Jr: Of the major Bush books published during the campaign season, *W: Revenge of The Bush Dynasty* by Elizabeth Mitchell (Hyperion: 370 pages) is fat and cautiously admiring; *First Son: George W. Bush* and the *Bush Family Dynasty* by Bill Minutaglio (Times Books: 371 pages) is fat, fawning and supercilious (both books are chock full of factoids devoid of political analysis and at best paint a portrait of an amiable sloath;) *Shrub: The Short but Happy Political Life of George W. Bush* by Molly Ivins and Lou Dubose (Random House: 179 pages) is thin with good red meat on its bones if you are of the inquiring mind-set to know if there is anything between hard covers to prove that George W. Bush Jr. is a no-goodnik.

On the secret world of mobsters, spooks and businessmen (not much about the Bush Family Business per se, but providing an insight into how such business is done: *In Banks We Trust* by Penny Lernoux (Doubleday, 1984); *The Crimes of Patriots: A True Tale of Dope, Dirty Money and The CIA* by Jonathan Kwitny (Norton, 1987); *Cocaine Politics* by Peter Dale Scott and Jonathan Marshall (Univ. of Calif. Press, 1991;) The truly classic *The Politics of Heroin in Southeast Asia* by Alfred W. McCoy (Harper and Row: 1972;) my personal (and hard to find) favorite is *The Great Heroin Coup: Drugs, Intelligence, and International Fascism* by Heinrick Kruger (South End Press, 1980.)

A general note on CIA books: Pay little heed to the vaunted classic on the CIA, *The Invisible Government*, which specializes in now-harmless exposes of CIA missteps while floating the apologia that the CIA is some run-amuk rogue elephant when in fact 9 1/2 times out of 10 the CIA is the agent to carry out covert policies of the executive branch of government positioned to make the executive capable of denying all knowledge if things go wrong, which they invariably do. A far superior basic book is *The CIA: A Forgotten History: U.S. Global Intervention Since World War II* by Walter Blum (Zed Books, London, 1986.) There is an updated U.S. edition which should be available through the Internet.

On the incredibly neglected S & L lynching by many of the players involved in the above captioned: *Inside Job: The Looting of America's Savings and Loans* by Stephen Pizzo, Mary Fricker and Paul Muolo (McGraw Hill: 1989;) and the somewhat histrionically titled but laboriously detailed *The Mafia, CIA & George Bush:The Untold Story of America's Greatest Financial Debacle* by Peter Brewton (Shaplosky Books, 1992.)

More if more is desired on George W. Bush Sr.'s well-buried major spook activities in *Deadly Secrets* by Hinckle and Turner (Thunder's Mouth, 1993.)

CHAPTER ONE:
Take Pride In Your Background

Texas is a place where people hold fast to basic values: give an honest day's work for an honest day's wages; don't lie, cheat, or steal; respect others their property, and respect their opinions.
—George W. Bush, "A Charge to Keep" (1999)

George W. Bush's stump speech is all tax cuts and Texas twang, all entrepreneurial zeal and assurances that his ZIP code is Austin, not Washington. So you'd never guess that his father, the former president, is distant kin to the queen of England. That his mother, Barbara Pierce Bush, shares bloodlines with President Franklin Pierce, the 14th man to run this country. That his grandfather Prescott Bush was a senator from Connecticut.
—Los Angeles Times, March 2, 2000

The biggest difference between me and my father is that he went to Greenwich Country Day and I went to San Jacinto Junior High.
—George W. Bush, Texas Monthly, April, 1989

For years, Bush has sought to play down his Eastern roots and his studies at the elite New England troika of Andover, Yale, and the Harvard Business School. Partly, it is because Bush seems reluctant to concede that he is anything but a Texan.
—Michael Kranish, Boston Globe, March 28, 1999

Although I was born in New Haven, Connecticut, while my dad was an undergraduate at Yale, we moved to West Texas when I was two. My first memories are of Midland.
—George W. Bush, "A Charge to Keep" (1999)

Bush and his advisers are trying to create a political mythology about his boyhood and early adult years in Midland. They describe the town as the incubator of the would-be president's egalitarianism, his belief in personal responsibility, and his philosophy of "compassionate conservatism." It's part of a larger effort to distinguish him from his father, who always suffered politically because of his image as a silver-spoon Yankee.
—Kenneth T. Walsh, U.S. News & World Report, June 7, 1999

Midland had a frontier feeling; it was hot and dry and dusty. We moved there in the midst of a long drought...tumbleweeds blew into our yard.
—George W. Bush, "A Charge To Keep" (1999)

Bush later wrote that the rising city on the plains could be called "Yuppieland West." Newly-laid out streets were named after Ivy League colleges. Millionaries lived along Harvard and Princeton Streets. They drove along Country Club Drive to socialize with others who were equally deep in the business of oil.
—Herbert S. Parmet, "George Bush: The Life of a Lone Star Yankee" (1997)

It was an unlikely place for George W to come of age, particularly since his parents were accustomed to the rarefied circles of the Eastern establishment. But for his father and the other young men who were drawn to West Texas in the late 1940's and early 1950's, the oil patch had its own exotic appeal.
—Texas Monthly, June 1999

There wasn't anything subtle or complicated about it. We all just wanted to make a lot of money quick.
—George Bush, "Looking Forward: An Autobiography" (1987)

Prosperity must have a greater purpose. The success of America has never been proven by cities of gold, but by citizens of character. Men and women

who work hard, dream big.
—George W. Bush, Cedar Rapids, Iowa, June 12, 1999

While Midland's oilmen have certainly exalted a laissez-faire system, their town has been both more elitist and less open to "the little guy" than the myth making allows. During Bush's time it was a white man's world, with little or no room for blacks or women at the top of the economic ladder. Business operators with pre-existing financial connections and good educations tended to do best. Working-class folks, in fact, tended not to live in Midland at all but to settle a few miles down Interstate 20 in Odessa.
—Kenneth T. Walsh, U.S. News & World Report, June 7, 1999

George W. grew up in a nice but unpretentious neighborhood with a bunch of brash, rough-and-tumble oilmen's sons—and he fit right in. Early photographs of George W. show a boy with a rakish gleam in his eye, an amused look on his face—"A wonderful, incorrigible child," says Barbara, "who spent many afternoons sitting in his room, waiting for his father to come home to speak to him about his latest transgression."
—Skip Hollandsworth, Texas Monthly, May 1994

Despite his latter-day reputation as a hell-raiser, Bush's worst offense as a kid was painting a false mustache on his face as a prank-for which the principal paddled his bottom.
—Kenneth T. Walsh, U.S. News & World Report, June 7, 1999

What rebellion he waged was stylistic. He became the real Texan in the family—chewing tobacco, using barnyard humor, settling the state's western corner—the one harboring what his aunt Nancy Ellis called a "slightly outrageous streak."
—Laurence I. Barrett, Time, July 31, 1989

While George was off at work, Bar was left alone in a strange town with no other focus but Georgie, who became in her words a "slightly spoiled little boy."
—Elizabeth Mitchell, "W: Revenge of the Bush Dynasty" (2000)

Few teachers or friends saw a great leader in their midst. "George was, well, an average guy in every way," says a friend from those days. "I mean that as a compliment."
—Kenneth T. Walsh, U.S. News & World Report, June 7, 1999

Andover was a serious place, and I took my studies seriously.
—George W. Bush, "A Charge To Keep" (1999)

Bush did not get off to an auspicious start when he arrived as at Phillips Academy in Andover, Mass., as a sophomore or "lower middler" in the school's vernacular. His first English grade —for an essay on emotions—was zero.
—Lois Romano, George Lardner Jr., Washington Post, July 27, 1999

Apparently Bush found the school's atmosphere a bit heavy. "I was able to instill a sense of frivolity." he said. "Andover was kind of a strange experience." Grateful for his organizational skills, classmates nicknamed him Tweeds Bush, after the classic backroom pol Boss Tweed.
—Texas Monthly, June 1999

At Andover, where his nicknames were "Lip" and "Tweeds," Bush was known as an "unexceptional student," as another classmate would later remember, who "played a lot of sports, none of them particularly well." In his senior year, he became head cheerleader.
—Paul Alexander, Rolling Stone, August 5, 1999

I loved sports...When I wasn't playing, I was an enthusiastic and spirited supporter of Yale's teams.
—George Bush, "A Charge to Keep" (1999)

Later in life, George W. would be forced to prove, and his friends would be at pains to explain, that male cheerleading wasn't for losers.
—Elizabeth Mitchell, "W: Revenge of the Bush Dynasty" (2000)

One yearbook photo shows Bush as head cheerleader, wielding a giant megaphone and wearing a sweater with a large "A." Another photo depicts Bush among several students trying to squeeze into a phone booth.
—Michael Kranish, Boston Globe, March 28, 1999

No one thought of him as a class leader in the traditional sense or had any inkling of the career he would ultimately choose.
—Lois Romano, George Lardner Jr., The Washington Post, July 27, 1999

CHAPTER THREE:
Take Pride In Your Background

In his early years, Bush followed his father's footsteps time and again, at Andover and at Yale, where, like his father, he was tapped for Skull and Bones the secretive club at Yale.
—Michael Kranish, Boston Globe, March 28, 1999

It was simply assumed that George W. was eventually going to be admit ted to Yale: his grandfather sat on Yale's board of trustees and his father had essentially left a legacy at Yale the equal of the one he had left at Andover.
—Bill Minutaglio, "First Son: George W. Bush and the Bush Family Dynasty" (1999)

Little George, as his friends at Yale preferred to call him, liked everybody on campus—every guy, that is, except the intellectual snobs.
—Elizabeth Mitchell, "W: Revenge of the Bush Dynasty" (2000)

"What angered me was the way such people at Yale felt so intellectually superior and so righteous," he says. "They thought they had all the answers."
—George W. Bush, Texas Monthly, May 1994

To hear Bush tell it, he was the last man with a crewcut in the last all-male class at Yale.
—Michael Kranish, Boston Globe, March 28, 1999

The atmosphere at Yale for most of my first three and half years was traditional.
—George W. Bush, "A Charge to Keep" (1999)

Bush clung to the traditions of an earlier era, boozy fraternity parties, secret societies and football weekends, while other classmates protested the war and challenged the political establishment that was waging it.
—Lois Romano, George Lardner Jr., The Washington Post, July 27, 1999

He recalls no protests against the war at Yale.
—Michael Kranish, Boston Globe, March 28, 1999

I was a senior at Yale in 1968, watching on TV as cities burned and people acted out their frustration and anger with violence...That's the way our genera tion learned about things.
—George W. Bush, Newsweek, June 21, 1999

George W. steered clear of the famous anti-war protests there. He majored in history, but he couldn't match his father's Phi Beta Kappa performance. One friend comments that he "didn't set the place on fire" but fell into "that broad middle." Actually, Bush was too busy partying to study.
–Paul Alexander, Rolling Stone, August 5, 1999

College was a time of hard work.
–George W. Bush, "A Charge to Keep" (1999)

The DKE house was...known as the jock-and-party fraternity, the place where the big men on campus would hang out...and almost everyone on campus knew that it had the biggest bar on campus...maybe the biggest bar in Connecticut.
–Bill Minutaglio, "First Son: George W. Bush and the Bush Family Dynasty" (1999)

Later, more than one friend would compare him to Otter in Animal House. Not only did he join Delta Kappa Epsilon, but he was elected president. Naturally, he wasn't averse to drinking.
—Paul Alexander, Rolling Stone, August 5, 1999

Bush is the first to say that he wasn't a great student or an intellectual.
—Michael Kranish, Boston Globe, March 28, 1999

He was the swashbuckling fraternity president, raw and fun, who people loved to be around. But unlike almost any other serious presidential candidate in modern memory, no one who knew him envisioned George W. Bush in the White House.
—Lois Romano, George Lardner Jr., The Washington Post, July 25, 1999

An era was ending and fun-loving preppies were falling out of step. In the fall of 1967, when huge numbers of college students were marching on Washington to protest the Vietnam War, Bush was quoted in the New York Times defending the branding of fraternity pledges with a hot coat hanger, saying the resulting wounds resembled "only a cigarette burn."
—Lois Romano, George Lardner Jr., The Washington Post, July 27, 1999

The charges against Delta Kappa Epsilon were made last Friday in a Yale Daily News article that accused campus fraternities of carrying on "sadistic and obscene" initiation procedures. The charges that has caused the most controversy on the Yale campus is that Delta Kappa Epsilon applied a "hot branding iron" to the small of the back of its 40 new members in ceremonies two weeks ago. A photograph showing a scab in the shape of the Greek letter Delta, approximately a half-inch wide appeared with the article. A former president of Delta claimed that the branding is done with a hot coathanger. But the former president, George Bush, a Yale senior, said that the resulting wound is "only a cigarette burn."
—Steve Weisman, New York Times, November 7, 1967

I was struck by the story of a gang initiation in Michigan. A 15-year-old boy was forced to stand and take two minutes of vicious beating from other members without fighting back. At the end, he was required to stand up and embrace his attackers. When asked why he submitted to this torture, he answered, "I knew this was going to hurt really bad, but I felt that if I could

ake it for just a couple of minutes, I'd be surrounded by people who loved
ne." Imagine a young life that empty, so desperately in need of real love.
–George W. Bush, Indianapolis, Indiana, July 22, 1999

**My senior year I joined Skull and Bones, a secret society, so secret I
can't say anything more.**
–George W. Bush, "A Charge to Keep" (1999)

The initiation into Skull & Bones, sometimes referred to as a process of dying
and being reborn, was considered a passport to adult privilege, 'converting the
dle progeny of the ruling class into morally serious leaders of the establish-
nent.'
–Bill Minutaglio, "First Son: George W. Bush and the Bush Family Dynasty"
(1999)

kull and Bones was Yale's most elite secret society...each young man was
equired to present his "PH" or personal history for the group as well as his
exual history.
–Lois Romano, George Lardner Jr., The Washington Post, July 27, 1999

**'ve already been asked by a reporter at a press conference, "Is it true
ou wrestled naked in a coffin at Skull and Bones [at Yale]?" he
ays...I'm not going to play their game. I've made mistakes, but I'm
going to bring honor, integrity, and dignity to the office.**
–George W. Bush, Texas Monthly, June 1999

I've always wanted to be a fighter pilot.
—George W. Bush, Press Release, Texas National Guard, March 24, 1970

One thing was still clear: most men entering the 147th Fighter Ring were under the impression they were not going to Vietnam.
—Bill Minutaglio, "First Son: George W. Bush and the Bush Family Dynasty" (1999)

"There was no question in my mind that I was going to serve—I was going to go to the military in 1968," Bush told U.S. News. "The question was, for me, what branch and when and how. And one of the things I made up my mind is I wanted to fly airplanes."
—U.S. News & World Report, November 1, 1999

He showed below-average potential as a would-be flier.
—Pete Slover, George Kuempel, The Dallas Morning News, September 4 1999

Bush said he was not given special help to get into the Guard—"They were having trouble getting people to volunteer to go to pilot school," he said—but his critics insist that strings had to have been pulled to get him in because former Guard officials have maintained that there was a long waiting list.
—Texas Monthly, June, 1999

Although the likelihood of his being accepted through standard channels was remote, Bush applied to the Guard during his last semester at Yale and was immediately admitted to the 147th Fighter Group of the Texas Air National Guard at Ellington Air Force Base in Houston, near the congressional district then represented by his father.
—Paul Alexander, Rolling Stone, August 5, 1999

Once he was in, Guard officials sought to capitalize on his standing as the son of a congressman. A 1970 Guard news release featured Mr. Bush as "one member of our younger generation who doesn't get his kicks from pot or hashish or speed. "Oh, he gets high, all right, but not from narcotics," it said.
—Pete Slover, George Kuempel, The Dallas Morning News, July 4, 1999

At the time I wanted to fight, yes, and I was willing to train for whatever experience came my way.
—George W. Bush, Boston Globe, March 28, 1999

Except for training periods in Georgia, Bush spent all of his time in Houston. He flew fighter jets for the Guard, but mostly he zipped around town in his sporty Triumph and partied.
—Paul Alexander, Rolling Stone, August 5, 1999

He played the role of fighter jock with considerable swagger, tucking a rakish orange scarf into his green flight suit, keeping his hair short and his shoes spit-shined. Always ready with a wisecrack and a smirk, the young lieutenant didn't take himself very seriously.
—Kenneth T. Walsh, U.S. News & World Report, November 1, 1999

One of Bush's favorite off-duty activities was pursuing the "aviation groupies" hanging around the bars and clubs near the base. He'd cruise by in his blue Triumph convertible, showing off a succession of impressive dates. And he loved carousing with the guys. The ritual was simple, according to a participant: Bellying up to the bar at a local tavern, someone in Bush's crowd would yell, "Dead bug," whereupon everyone would drop to the floor, flop onto his back, and twitch his arms and legs. The last one to hit the ground would have to buy the next round.
—Kenneth T. Walsh, U.S. News & World Report, November 1, 1999

Mr. Bush said he took flying seriously. "You will die in your airplane if you didn't practice, and I wasn't interested in dying," he said.
—Pete Slover, George Kuempel, The Dallas Morning News, September 4, 1999

Veterans groups angrily criticized Bush for comparing the risk he faced flying jets on practice runs over Texas to the risk American soldiers faced in live combat in Vietnam
—Texas Monthly, June 1999

Mr. Bush's application for the Guard included a box to be checked specifying whether he did or did not volunteer for over-seas duty. His includes a check mark in the box not wanting to volunteer for such an assignment.
—Pete Slover, George Kuempel, The Dallas Morning News, July 4, 1999

When I ask him if he tried to avoid the draft, he grins and says, "Hell, no. Do you think I'm going to admit that? You are out of your mind. Let me give you the political answer, Mr. Reporter"—and then he tells me he wasn't dodging anything.
—Skip Hollandsworth, Texas Monthly, May 1994

He didn't go to Canada to dodge the draft because, as one of his best friends and closest fraternity brothers would suggest, he was worried about destroying his father's plans for the Senate and beyond.
—Bill Minutaglio, "First Son: George W. Bush and the Bush Family Dynasty" (1999)

True courage, it's said, is the most generous of the virtues. It elevates ideals over self and duty over comfort. It leads young men and women to risk everything they have, everything they value.
—George W. Bush speech, Veterans Day, Manchester, New Hampshire, November 10, 1999

CHAPTER FIVE:
Honor your Father's Achievements

My Dad does have a wealth of knowledge and experience.
—George W. Bush, "A Charge to Keep" (1999)

"Are you going to write that kind of article?" he asks me, his voice getting edgy.
"One of those pseudo-psychological me-and-my-Dad stories?"
—Skip Hollandsworth, Texas Monthly, May 1994

Of the five Bush children, George, the eldest, (has) always been the most
drawn to Dad's patterns of endeavors.
—Laurence I. Barrett, Time, July 31, 1989

In his early years, Bush followed his father's footsteps time and again.
—Michael Kranish, Boston Globe, March 28, 1999

If one superimposes a timeline over the Bush career path, one sees that
his rise in business coincided with his father's rise to the highest levels of
government.
—Bryon York, The American Spectator, June 1999

Why don't I talk about my father? Because I'm (the one) running for president.
—George W. Bushy, Houston Chronicle, December 10, 1999

While bristling at the suggestion that he is merely riding his father's
coattails, Mr. Bush — a spitting image of the president—concedes his
name has opened some political doors.
—Wall Street Journal; New York; April 3, 1989

When asked to compare his faith with his father's, the affability drains from
Bush's voice, "You're going to have to figure that out for yourself." But the
subtext is clear: There is a gulf between us.
—Franklin Foer, U.S. News & World Report, December 6, 1999

"People want to hear and feel and see what the president's son is all
about," he says with a distinct Texas twang. "The downside is that I will
be judged unfairly by some people. Some people will say, 'You're running
on your daddy's name.'"
—Wall Street Journal; New York; April 3, 1989

My problem was "What's the boy ever done?" I have to make a fairly big splash in the pool in order for people to recognize me.
—George W. Bush, Newsday, May 8, 1989

In short, Bush is by and large a politician without a political identity. This lack of identity is explained in part by his political origins, in part by his survival instincts. He was moved to enter politics more by the service tradition of his family and social class than by passion for any cause or an idea.
—George Bush: Fighting The Wimp Factor," Newsweek, October 19, 1987

He would never be called wimp. He was, they whispered, more like Ronald Reagan. He had that cock-of-the-walk way about him. He seemed more peppery Texan than flighty preppy.
—Maureen Dowd, New York Times, February 16, 2000

My father was the guy, a great World War II hero, who was branded a wimp at one time. I understand the labeling that goes on in the political process.

The shadows of his father's successes are never far from George W...should he achieve this goal, he will finally be able to say that he is just as successful as his father.
—Texas Monthly, June 1999

Look, having the name "George Bush" opened some doors. But it closed some, too. And the name brings with it the burden of high expectations-very high. That's the challenge for me now: to see if I can meet or even exceed those expectations.
—George W. Bush, Newsweek, June 21, 2000

In this, he is a true Bush—his father's son down to a fierce desire to win for the sake of winning.
—Richard Cohen, The Washington Post, February 25, 2000

"All that I ask," he says, giving me another glare, "is that for once you guys stop seeing me as the son of George Bush."
—Skip Hollandsworth, Texas Monthly, May 1994

Being George Bush's son has its pluses, and it had its minuses.
—George W. Bush, Newsweek, January 24, 2000

If Al Gore is stiff because his father always expected him to be president, perhaps W. is loose because his father never expected him to be president.
—Maureen Dowd, New York Times, October 6, 1999

Decades ago, George Herbert Walker and his daughter Dorothy Walker had instilled the ferocious sense of competition on one side of the family—their belief that life was essentially broken down into a constant series of competitions that needed to be won at all costs.
—Bill Minutaglio, "First Son: George W. Bush and the Bush Family Dynasty" (1999)

His mother gave him her tart tongue and free spirit.
—Skip Hollandsworth, Texas Monthly, May 1994

"George W. says he got his mother's mouth." A prominent Republican is less kind: "Barbara Bush is an exceedingly vindictive, nasty individual with a very high opinion of herself. She's always been that way." Cocky, boisterous, flippant - these were the traits George W. was developing as a young man.
—Paul Alexander, Rolling Stone, August 5, 1999

"Sometimes I maybe stepped over the line in terms of civility," he continued. "People shouldn't have taken that personally. And I evidently developed a reputation as somebody who was quick with the quip. Maybe the Barbara Bush in me was coming out. "
—George W. Bush, New York Times, October 6, 1999

He will inevitably be compared to his father, but he is more like his mother. "His personality and temperament come from Barbara," says Laura Bush. "They both love to needle."
—Texas Monthly, June 1999

He was more like Bar, the way he called a spade a spade. But he'd learned some control as he'd neared the age of forty
—Richard Ben Cramer, "What It Takes" (1992)

Momma tells me not to say that and Dad tells me not to say this. I am 40-some years old and they're still telling me what to do.
—George W. Bush, Texas Monthly, June 1999

This is very important, you might want to write this down—I have learned that, no matter how old you are or what you do, you can never escape your mother.
—George W. Bush, Mission High School Graduation, Mission, TX, May 29, 1998

"This is what happened," Roger Stone says. "George W. used to be more like his mother, but over time he became more like his father. He matured."
—Wall Street Journal, New York; April 3, 1989

My first goal is to usher in the responsibility era. An era that stands in stark contrast to the last few decades, when the culture has clearly said: If it feels good, do it.
—George W. Bush, Latin Business Association Luncheon, September 2, 1999

I don't know why I drank. I liked to drink, I guess.
—George W. Bush, Washington Post, July 25, 1999

If not clinically an alcoholic, Bush sometimes came close to the line. Sometimes he would embarrass himself; more often, he didn't know how to stop.
—Lois Romano, George Lardner, Jr., The Washington Post, July 25, 1999

Drinking also magnified aspects of my personality that probably don't need to be larger than they already are—made me more funny, more charming (I thought), more irrepressible.
—George W. Bush, "A Charge to Keep" (1999)

One evening Bush went drinking with his youngest brother, Marvin, who was then just fifteen. On the way back to his parents' house he drove over a neighbor's trash can. When his father asked him to step into the den to talk about what happened, Bush snapped, "You want to go mano a mano right here?" Some believe the incident symbolized the sons need to stand up to his far more successful father, but not Bush. "It was probably the result of two stiff bourbons, nothing more," he told me with a wry smile.
—Skip Hollandsworth, Texas Monthly, June 1999

Then there's the rumor that there is a photo—out there somewhere — depicting the governor in his younger days dancing naked on top of a bar. The photo has been written about in the Star tabloid, and its existence has been hinted at on the Internet.
—Ellen Joan Pollock, Wall Street Journal, May 14, 1999

Note to Jay Leno and other comedians who have had so much fun with the George-Bush-danced-naked-on-a-bar rumor. It's not true. The toga costume is about as close as you are going to get.
—George W. Bush, "A Charge to Keep" (1999)

A charismatic partier since his school days, Bush liked to drink what he called the four Bs—beer, bourbon and B&B. But he had begun to realize that his drinking was jeopardizing his relationships, his career and his health.
—Lois Romano, George Lardner, Jr., The Washington Post, July 25, 1999

I would tend to talk too much when drinking. If you're feisty anyway, you don't need any reason to be more feisty.
—George W. Bush, Time, July 31, 1989

He confronted the problem once and for all during a three-day weekend in late July 1986 at the Broadmoor, a grand old resort in Colorado Springs. The Bushes and their closest friends had gone there to escape the Oil Patch and celebrate a communal 40th-birthday party.
—Eric Pooley, Time, June 21, 1999

"It was a party," said Joe O'Neill. "We were all sort of loud, and George gets louder than most. You know, we were that loud table in the corner of the restaurant. And I think in my heart that it dawned on him, or Laura said to him, that he could end up doing something to embarrass his father, and that just did it." George W. went cold turkey the next morning.
—Paul Alexander, Rolling Stone, August 5, 1999

Bush turned 40, gave up drinking and became what he describes as a born-again Christian.
—Los Angeles Times, March 2, 1999

Addicts become examples. Reckless men become loving fathers. Prisoners become spiritual leaders- sometimes more mature and inspiring than many of us can ever hope to be.
—George W. Bush, Indianapolis, Indiana, July 22, 1999

Over time, Bush replaced his drinking with a near-addiction to jogging and a new devotion to Laura's Methodist religion - a faith much more evangelical than the Episcopal Church he'd grown up in.
—Paul Alexander, Rolling Stone; August 5, 1999

His recommitment to Jesus Christ — "is one of the defining moments of my life. But I do so understanding that I am a lowly sinner as well."
—George W. Bush, New York Times, January 23, 2000

CHAPTER EIGHT:
Ask Forgiveness For Your Indiscretions

Children who corrupt their wills and souls with drugs...These are burdens on the conscience of a successful nation.
—Governor George W. Bush, Cedar Rapids, Iowa, June, 12, 1999

George Walker Bush is one member of the younger generation who doesn't get his kicks from pot or hashish or speed. Oh, he gets high, all right, but not from narcotics...as far as kicks are concerned, Lt. Bush gets his from the roaring afterburner of the F-102.
—Press Release, Office of Information, Texas National Guard, March 24, 1970

During the 1994 governor's race, he brusquely told the Houston Chronicle, "Maybe I did [use drugs], maybe I didn't.... How I behaved as an irresponsible youth is irrelevant to this campaign.... What matters is how I behave as an adult."
—Texas Monthly, June 1999

Bush...has created something of a political monster...spawning countless rumors that have him doing everything from dancing naked on a bar to copping cocaine on a Washington street. "I'm amazed at how one simple statement has set off a swirl —that I'm the wildest man that ever lived," Bush said.
—Lois Romano and George Lardner Jr., The Washington Post, July 25, 1999

People familiar with the social scene in Houston at that time say cocaine was often used by affluent, young singles, but there is no evidence that Bush took the drug himself.
—Kenneth T. Walsh, U.S. News & World Report, November 1, 1999

A gossip-circuit favorite: that Mr. Bush, the top contender for the Republican presidential nomination, bought coke on a Washington street corner and was high at his father's inauguration.
—Ellen Joan Pollock, Wall Street Journal, May 14, 1999

"He's said he did some things that are bad, but what's bad? Heroin?" says a friend who has known Bush since college. "He didn't do heroin. Grass is not a big deal anymore - is it?" But at the time, some people close to Bush believed his indulgent lifestyle-was a big deal, among them his father.
—Paul Alexander, Rolling Stone, August 5, 1999

I happen to think Bush is a Fifth Amendment cokehead. If he had not used the stuff, he would certainly say so. After all, it's not as if he is such a reticent fellow. He has told us much about his past — his drinking, his carousing, his lost youth, his meandering career path and how he gave up booze and found God...what, if anything, has Bush learned from the life he once led? Why, for instance, does he think that people who use cocaine recreationally ought to go to jail?
—Richard Cohen, Washington Post, August 19, 1999

Countless thousands of people are rotting in prisons all across America - many in Texas - for being caught with small amounts of cocaine or crack, its smokable variant. Many were only peripherally involved in drug sales. Some were mere users. As governor of Texas, Bush - like most other politicians in both parties - has joined in this orgy of punishment with enthusiasm, signing laws that toughen penalties for drug users as well as pushers, and that send juveniles as young as 14 to prison for especially serious crimes, including some drug crimes.
—Stuart Taylor Jr., Newsweek, August 30, 1999

We must teach our children...We must instill in them the courage to resist the lure of drugs — to stand up and say: "Absolutely not. I will not buy your drugs. I will not sell them. I will not fall for the lie that drugs are hip and vogue. Because I know that drugs will destroy me."
—George W. Bush, Mission High School Graduation, Mission, TX, May 29, 1998

Because he was a rich white kid with an important daddy, Bush's chances of going to prison for drug use were nil. Yet there is no recognition anywhere in his record of "There but for the grace of God go I." In fact, to the contrary, Bush has acted to make sure that poor folks have even less access to justice in the system.
—Molly Ivins and Lou Dubose, "W: The Short But Happy Life of George W. Bush" (2000)

There is a disparity between the way rich kids and big shots and suburbanites get treated when they are caught with cocaine, and the way poor people are treated when they get caught with crack. And as Time notes this week: "If Bush did try cocaine, how does that square with his support of Texas legislation putting those caught with less than a gram of the drug in jail?"
—Maureen Dowd, New York Times, August 18, 1999

I've told people I've learned from my mistakes—and I have.
—George W. Bush, Washington Post, July 25, 1999

Not only could I pass the background check and the standards applied to today's White House, but I could have passed the background check and the standards applied on the most stringent conditions when my dad was president of the United States.
—George W. Bush, Houston Chronicle, August 20, 1999

Federal disclosure requirements developed by President Bush's White House required that applicants say if they had used drugs since they were 18 years old...But Bush, 53, drew a line at an afternoon news conference in Columbus, Ohio, and adamantly refused to discuss whether he used drugs before 1974, when he was 28. "I told the American people all I am going to tell them," Bush said.
—Bennett Roth, R.G. Ratcliffe, Alan Bernstein, Houston Chronicle, August 20, 1999

There are right choices in life and wrong choices in life. Drugs will destroy you. Alcohol will ruin your life....Some people think it's inappropriate to draw a moral line. Not me.
—Governor George W. Bush, Cedar Rapids, Iowa, June, 12, 1999

CHAPTER NINE:
Don't Flaunt Your Intelligence

Rarely is the question asked: Is our children learning?
—George W. Bush, Florence, South Carolina, January 11, 2000

George is no dummy. He's a smart fellow.
—Barbara Bush, Dallas Morning News, December 3, 1999

A mediocre student, Bush majored in history, with grades that were apparently not good enough for admission to the University of Texas law school, which turned him down as an in-state applicant two years after he graduated. Bush has not given permission to either Andover or Yale to release his grades.
—Lois Romano, George Lardner Jr., Washington Post, July 27, 1999

Bush, ever the wisecracking fun lover, was the life of the party but never struck many friends as particularly altruistic or brilliant.
—Kenneth T. Walsh, U.S. News & World Report, November 1, 1999

The creeping notion and allegations, spread by Democrats in Texas, (is) that George W. Bush never had the patience or the discipline to study policy, that he suffered from some sort of attention deficit, that he was ...bordering on being an outright anti-intellectual.
—Bill Minutaglio, "First Son: George W. Bush and the Bush Family Dynasty" (1999)

In some ways Bush comes across as the opposite of his father, President George Bush, a cerebral, worldly man of great experience who knew everything except how to be folksy. The younger Bush once confessed that his greatest weakness is his lack of interest in long books, especially those about policy, and that the only statistics he seems to know involve baseball.
—Nicholas D. Kristof, New York Times, March 5, 2000

Bush himself fueled the image that he is the "lite" version of his father by his enthusiastic dismissals of all things intellectual. He told Talk Magazine that he is bad at "sitting down and reading a 500-page book on public policy or philosophy or something." He told The National Journal: "I won't read treatises. I'll read summaries."
—R.G. Ratcliffe, Houston Chronicle, December 5, 1999

We are a national where a majority of fourth-graders in our cities can't read or understand a simple book."
—George W. Bush, "A Charge to Keep" (1999)

An elementary school pupil in South Carolina asked Bush to name his favorite book as a child, and he could think of none.
—R.G. Ratcliffe, Houston Chronicle, December 5, 1999

Whenever George W. Bush is challenged about failing to take a moral position, he responds by saying, 'Don't judge my heart.' OK. Let's judge his brain.
—Richard Cohen, Washington Post, February 25, 2000

Gov. George W. Bush was hit with a surprise quiz on foreign affairs Wednesday. His score: 25 percent. The GOP presidential front-runner, interviewed by WHDH-TV, the NBC affiliate in Boston, was asked to name the leaders of four current world hot spots: Chechnya, Taiwan, India and Pakistan. He was able to give a partial response to one: Taiwan.
—Associated Press, November 5, 1999

After he had failed a reporter's pop quiz last fall about foreign leaders, including the name of the Indian prime minister, Mr. Bush winced today when a moderator mentioned the words "pop quiz." Jokingly, Mr. Bush dared the moderator to ask him the name of the Indian president. "Do you know who the president of India is?" the moderator asked obligingly. "Vajpayee," Mr. Bush said, grinning and looking pleased with himself. But Atal Behari Vajpayee is the prime minister of India; the president is K. R. Narayanan.
—New York Times, February 26, 2000

After a rally in Canton, Mich., last week, a man posing as a Canadian television reporter told Mr. Bush that Canadian Prime Minister Jean Poutine had endorsed him as "the man to lead the free world into the 21st century." Mr. Bush beamed. "I'm honored," he said. "I appreciate his strong statement," the aspiring president added, "He understands our belief in free trade..." Unfortunately for Mr. Bush, Canada's prime minister is Jean Chretien, not Poutine. Poutine is a French-Canadian concoction of french fries and cheese curds smothered in gravy that is much beloved in Quebec. The man posing as a journalist was Canadian comedian Rick Mercer, whose segment on a satirical weekly TV show often lampoons American ignorance of Canadian matters.
—Wall Street Journal, March 2, 2000

Is George W. Bush not the sharpest knife in the drawer? We know he doesn't know Slovakia from Slovenia, Greeks from "Grecians," or that there is no "standard" version of the Ten Commandments. And we also know that the big bookshelf in his Austin office contains baseballs and not books. Typically, however, Bush is unfazed. "Just because I happen to mispronounce the name of a country doesn't mean that I don't understand how to lead," he says...It is revealing that the Bush campaign does not make any great claims as to Bush's intellect.
—Roger Simon, U.S. News & World Report, July 19, 1999

Imagine the CEO of your company not knowing who runs the second largest company in his industry. That's what it looked like when Bush didn't know who runs the second largest country in the world, India (which will pass China soon and become the world's most populous nation). Luckily for Bush, the voters haven't tuned in yet. Unluckily for him, when they do, a gentleman's C might not cut it.
—Jonathan Alter, Newsweek, November 22, 1999

When he stumbles over abstruse matters of foreign policy, for instance, he actually jokes about his cluelessness...this is how frat boys behave when they know the class nerd is going to take their exams for them.
–Tony Snow, Denver Post, November 14, 1999

Gov. George W. Bush has proved that he inherited the ability of his father, former President George Bush, to mangle the English language. While speaking Friday night to a crowd at Iowa Western Community College in Council Bluffs, the Republican front-runner strained the native tongue trying to describe how in the post-Cold War world the United States can no longer focus on the Soviet Union as its enemy. "When I was coming up, it was a dangerous world and you knew exactly who the they were. It was us vs. them, and it was clear who them was. Today we're not so sure who the they are, but we know they're there," Bush said to snickers from the audience.
–R.G. Ratcliffe, Houston Chronicle, January 23, 2000

Such slips are understandable; none is a flogging offense. However, having committed them, Bush should take care not to exacerbate the suspicion that he has a seriousness deficit.
–George Will, Washington Post, August 12, 1999

Marilyn Quayle accused Bush of being the truly empty vessel in the race, a man towed through life by his famous father, former President George Bush. "The caricature they made of Dan in '88 is George W," she said. "It's him. It wasn't true about Dan. But it is him." According to her, "(Bush) is the guy that never accomplished anything, everything he got Daddy took care of," adding that her husband's rival was "the party frat-boy type."
–Arizona Republic, July 26, 1999

I'm very gracious and humbled."
–George W. Bush, This Week With Cokie Roberts, February 20, 2000

America doesn't like intellectuals and policy wonks any more than Bush does. If he simply gets the votes of anyone who has ever thrown a paper airplane in class or not studied for a test, he'll win in a landslide.
–Jonathan Alter, Newsweek, November 22, 1999

Wealth is created by Americans—by creativity and enterprise and risk-taking.
—George W. Bush, Cedar Rapids, Iowa, June 12, 1999

After finishing Harvard Business School, Bush headed south to his boyhood
home of Midland, in Texas' resource-rich Permian Basin, to make his way in the
oil business like his father had done nearly 30 years before.
—Los Angeles Times, March 2, 2000

**The contention is that he exploited his family contacts to get advantages
no one else had, and at least part of the critique is true. He started in
Midland with about $17,000 from an educational trust provided by his
parents. And family friends invested several hundred thousand dollars in
his fledgling oil business, some persuaded by Jonathan Bush, his uncle, a
stockbroker in New York.**
—Kenneth T. Walsh, U.S. News & World Report, June 7, 1999

Because federal tax laws made oil companies good tax shelters, Bush had no
trouble getting investors for Arbusto...Most of Arbusto's investors were friends
and associates of George W.'s father, whose attempt to win the Republican
presidential nomination in 1980 ended with Ronald Reagan putting him on the
ticket as his vice president.
—Paul Alexander, Rolling Stone, August 5, 1999

**"My father's name helped me attract early investors for my business," the
former president said in response to written questions submitted by The
Washington Post. "If my name did the same for ` W,' great!**
—Washington Post, July 30, 1999

Like his father he chose a Spanish name for it: Arbusto Energy Inc. "Arbusto" is
Spanish for "bush"; the president's company was Zapata Petroleum Co.
—Wall Street Journal, December 6, 1991

Arbusto became Bush Exploration. Company officials believed having "Bush"
in the title would attract more investors than a firm with an obscure Spanish
allusion to the owner's name.
—Byron York, The American Spectator, June 1999

Despite the new name, the public offering failed. According to Securities and
Exchange Commission documents, Bush intended to raise $6 million but
brought in just $1.3 million. To make matters worse, the wells he drilled either

were dry or produced little oil, and investors lost seventy-five percent of their money.
—Paul Alexander, Rolling Stone, August 5, 1999

Texas is Texas because of dreamers and doers who took big risks and failed miserably.
—George W. Bush, Mission High Graduation, Mission, TX, May 29, 1998

The company was absorbed by Spectrum 7, another rinky-dink oil company bankrolled by Reagan-Bush types. It, too, was a failure
—Robert Sherrill, Texas Monthly, July 1999

As the hard times continued, Spectrum merged with Harken Energy. Harken viewed Mr. Bush's famous name as an important asset.
—Micah Morrison, Wall Street Journal, September 28, 1999

I understand small business growth. I was one.
--- George W. Bush, New York Daily News, February 19, 2000

The deal, finished in September 1986, brought him a large amount of Harken stock, worth at least $500,000 at the time, plus a consulting contract that paid him as much as $120,000 a year.
—Byron York, The American Spectator, June 1999

Records show that the company's stock began to climb right after the Spectrum merger was announced, hitting $6 a share within a year before falling back. Mr. Bush was philosophical about losing his management role in the oil business but retaining profit. "I try to talk up Harken whenever I can," he told Forbes magazine in June 1987, "and I'd feel a lot worse if the stock hadn't tripled."
—Micah Morrison, Wall Street Journal, September 28, 1999

In January 1990, with shares trading around $4.50, Harken announced that it had signed a potentially lucrative oil-exploration deal with the government of Bahrain.
—Kevin Sack, New York Times, May 9, 1999

When the country's rulers handed Harken that deal early last year, it puzzled oil experts around the world. Why would Bahrain stake so much of its financial future on an obscure, money-losing company with no refineries and no experience in off-shore oil exploration?
—Richard Behar, Time, October 28, 1991

The speculations are that when Bahrain's rulers awarded a high-stakes oil deal to Harken Energy, they were trying to win favors from the White House. Pres Bush's oldest son, George W. Bush, is a Harken investor, director and consultant.
—Time, July 31, 1989

Harken says it won the Bahrain drilling deal purely on merit, through painstaking geological research and deft negotiating. It says Mr. Bush played no role in clinching the deal.
—Wall Street Journal, December 6, 1991

When the Bahrain contract was made public, Harken's stock jumped in value, and he (Bush) sold 212,140 shares-60 percent of his holdings- for $848,500. **Nice timing.**
—Robert Sherrill, Texas Monthly, July 1999

Eight days after Bush's stock sale, Harken wound up its second quarter with operating losses from day-to-day activities of $6.7 million...Iraq's invasion of Kuwait stirred fears that it would endanger a potentially lucrative offshore drilling contract with Bahrain.
—George Lardner Jr., Lois Romano, Washington Post, July 30, 1999

It's possible, even likely, that President Bush, loaded with C.I.A. data, warned him of the coming crisis. Did George W. sell because he had this exclusive, insider information that wasn't available to the public? That would have been a violation of Securities and Exchange Commission regulations.
—Robert Sherrill, Texas Monthly, July 1999

Mr. Bush ultimately was cleared by the Securities and Exchange Commission. But suspicions of Mr. Bush's lucky timing had heightened at first, when the SEC, discovering that he had not filed the proper disclosure form, opened an investigation into the president's son.
—Micah Morrison, Wall Street Journal; September 28, 1999

It was widely assumed that Bush, a director of the company, had insider knowledge and dumped his stock in advance of the bad news.
—Eric Pooley, Time, June 21, 1999

Reporters have been particularly intrigued by George W.'s adventure in the oil industry, and well they might be. There was something about it that smacked of a shell game run by a very fast hand.
—Robert Sherrill, Texas Monthly, July 1999

Even now, questions linger about a 1990 sale of Harken stock by Bush that was the subject of a probe by the Securities and Exchange Commission.
—George Lardner Jr., Lois Romano, Washington Post, July 30, 1999

Defeat humbles you.
—George W. Bush, "A Charge to Keep" (1999)

In 1978, again like his father, he made an early, unsuccessful run for Congress. His Democratic opponent, Kent Hance, tagged Bush as a Connecticut carpet-bagger.
—Michael Kranish, Boston Globe, March 28, 1999

Bush took conservative positions on touchstone issues—he believed the Equal Rights Amendment was "unnecessary"; he opposed the use of federal funds for abortions; he said he had "done nothing to promote homosexuality in our society"—and he reminded Republicans that they should run him in November because he had "proven he can raise money."
—Paul Alexander, Rolling Stone, August 5, 1999

Hance made Bush's money another liability, claiming that much of it came from out of the district.
—Molly Ivins and Lou Dubose, "Shrub" (2000)

His father, who was eyeing a White House bid, held fund-raisers for George W. in Washington, Houston, Dallas and Midland, Texas.
—Los Angeles Times, March 2, 2000

Hance and his allies attacked Bush as a rich Northeastern prep-school brat who didn't understand "Texas values."
—Kenneth T. Wals, U.S. News & World Report, Washington, June 7, 1999

(Bush) refused to allow his father to campaign for him that year. When one primary opponent called him "Junior," Mr. Bush began taking his birth certificate to speeches to prove he and his father had different middle names.
—Robert Tomsho, Wall Street Journal, April 3, 1989

During the campaign, he repeatedly said he had only one regret—that he hadn't been born in Texas.
—Bill Minutaglio, "First Son: George W. Bush and the Bush Family Dynasty" (1999)

I'm proud of what my father has accomplished and I'm proud of my education, but I have spent half my life in West Texas and this is my home.
—George W. Bush Odessa American, October 25, 1978

When Hance got through with him, Bush smelled like some exotic houseplant on a New England windowsill...Bush lost, 47% to 53%. Never again would he let a rival paint him as an elitist.
—Eric Pooley, Time, June 21, 1999

In his losing bid for Congress in 1978, he learned two political lessons that he never forgot: Hit back hard when attacked, and hammer home a strong, clear message.
—Kenneth T. Walsh, U.S. News & World Report, June 7, 1999

It's hard not to take a political loss personally; after all, it's your own name spelled out there on the ballot. Yet if you believe in the wisdom of the voters, as I do, you get over the disappointment, accept the verdict, and move on.
—George W. Bush, "A Charge to Keep" (1999)

CHAPTER TWELVE:
Make Money The Old Fashioned Way

There's no question that I am a blessed person. I was blessed by a family that gave me unconditional love.
—George W. Bush, Newsweek; June 21, 1999

If it weren't for 'preferential treatment,' George W. Bush's only way of becoming seriously rich would have been if he won the lottery—or played the futures market. As it happened, he didn't have to. He hit his number at birth.
—Richard Cohen, Washington Post, November 7, 1999

Prosperity is not a given.
—George W. Bush, Cedar Rapids, Iowa, June 12, 1999

Like the Kennedys, the Bush offspring inherited power bases in politics and among the moneyed elite. Like the Kennedys, they have not hesitated, for money and political support, to cozy up to some operators who played fast and loose, to put it mildly.
—Robert Sherrill, Texas Monthly, July 1999

We're all equal in God's eyes. And all of our citizens must know they have an equal chance to succeed.
—George W. Bush,
Inauguration Speech,
1994

George W. is comfortable with being a child of wealth and fame. He doesn't feel guilty when he cashes in on family connections to cut business deals or raise campaign cash.
—Business Week,
November 15, 1999

I know how hard it is for you to put food on your family.
—George W. Bush, New Hampshire, January 27, 2000

Access to the rich and famous, of course, isn't available to everyone. But Bush and his father see no reason to apologize for it.
—George Lardner, Jr., Lois Romano, The Washington Post, July 30, 1999

Mr. Bush has collected a rather rich assortment of connections in his career as the son of a man who was president, vice president and director of the Central Intelligence Agency. His personal financial position seems secure, thanks in no small way to friends of his father.
—**Micah Morrison, Wall Street Journal, September 28, 1999**

Bush angrily denied any collusion or conflicts of interest, saying, "I didn't—I swear I didn't—get into politics to feather my nest or feather my friends' nests...Any insinuation that I have used my office to help my friends is simply not true."
—Houston Chronicle, August 12, 1998

After the (presidential) campaign, George W. Bush moved into the White House transition team, making sure that only the Bush faithful were rewarded with prized jobs in the new administration.
—**Gilbert A. Lewthwaite, The Baltimore Sun, December 15, 1991**

More than 4,000 donors who gave money to support President Bush's failed reelection bid also donated to his son's current electoral effort...the father received $3.8 million from the 4,201 joint donors, while the son received nearly $4.1 million.
—The Los Angeles Times, March 2, 2000

The best policy for campaign reform is to let the sun shine in.
—George W. Bush, Houston Chronicle, July 1, 1999

115 fund-raisers are called "Pioneers" because they are blazing new trails in campaign finance by raising at least $100,000 each for his Republican presidential bid. The fund-raisers and Bush's campaign insist that the money is a result of a populist grass-roots campaign, not the work of elite business leaders seeking favors.
—**R.G. Ratcliffe, Alan Bernstein, Houston Chronicle, July 21, 1999**

Americans will never write the epitaph of idealism. It emerges from our nature as a people, with a vision of the common good beyond profit and loss.
—George W. Bush, Indianapolis, Indiana, July 22, 1999

Just as father Joseph Kennedy showed his political brood how the Mafia could be useful, father George Bush provided entrée to a corrupt bureaucracy.
—Robert Sherrill, Texas Monthly, July 1999

Eight of the Pioneers are people who helped the governor's father, George Bush, win the presidency in 1988 by donating $100,000 or more of their own money to the Republican National Committee, a feat that granted them membership to Team 100. At least two were criticized for getting special favors from the Bush administration.
—R.G. Ratcliffe, Alan Bernstein, Houston Chronicle, July 21, 1999

Money doesn't win. It's a pretty good start.
—George W. Bush, Houston Chronicle, July 1, 1999

His silver-spoon lineage apparently hasn't made him less credible with working-class Republicans on issues such as welfare and public education, GOP analysts said. "I think you can be totally compassionate and totally rich," Republican pollster (Christine L.) Matthews.
—Alexis Simendinger, National Journal, September 6, 1997

And for selflessness: not in there to make money, not in there to end up in a position where you can just influence your own future.
—George W. Bush, Newsweek, June 21, 1999

The Pioneers...are dyspeptic over the Prodigal Son. They don't understand how their Boy could have gone through $60 million of the nest egg they built. It was supposed to buy the White House, not one measly caucus and one lousy primary. How on earth did Junior hemorrhage more than a million dollars per delegate? Did he think it was a trust fund
—Maureen Dowd, New York Times, February 27, 2000

The record of Bush's rise to wealth reveals how he became what he is today. It's a complicated tale of family connections, hard work, and sweet deals, topped off by a taxpayer-subsidized baseball bonanza that may leave some Republicans feeling queasy about how their candidate got rich.
—Byron York, The American Spectator, June 1999

(Bush) spied two well-heeled lobbyists walking down the steps among the throngs of tourists. He rolled down his window and shouted, "Show me the money!" They obediently flashed their wallets. One can only imagine what the common folk thought of this byplay.
—Texas Monthly; June 1999

I'm very comfortable now with who I am.
—George W. Bush, New York Times, May 9, 1999

CHAPTER THIRTEEN:
Go To Bat For Others

I live in the moment, seize opportunities, and try to make the most of them."
—George W. Bush, "A Charge to Keep" (1999)

How Mr. Bush parlayed a lackluster tenure in the oil patch into a $15 million home run and a seat in the governor's mansion is a subtle morality tale about the highways and byways to contemporary political power. Micah Morrison, Wall Street Journal, September 28, 1999

As everyone knows, George W. used $600,000 from the Harken stock sale to buy a tiny slice of the Texas Rangers; and when the Rangers were sold last year for $250 million, the second-largest amount ever paid for a baseball team, George W. emerged with more than $14.9 million.
—Robert Sherrill, Texas Monthly, July 1999

Bush acknowledges that his name and connections played a major role in his success. "Look, I don't deny it. How could I?" he says. "Being George Bush's son has its pluses and negatives."
—Eric Pooley, Time; June 21, 1999

Privilege, pedigree, and personal relationships were the reasons Bush hooked up with the Rangers in the first place. His name surfaced as a possible major league owner in the weeks after his father was elected president.
—Texas Monthly, June 1999

The seller, Eddie Chiles, was an old friend of President Bush and he wanted to sell to George W.
—Richard Cohen, Washington Post, November 7, 1999

I had nowhere near the $80 million it would take to purchase the team. I am, however, a hard worker who catches a dream and refuses to let go."
—George W. Bush, "A Charge to Keep" (1999)

Baseball Commissioner Peter Ueberroth stepped in, brokering a deal that brought Fort Worth financier Richard Rainwater together with the Bush group. Mr. Ueberroth's pitch to Mr. Rainwater was that he join the deal partly "out of respect" for President Bush, a source close to the negotiations told the New York Times.
—Micah Morrison, Wall Street Journal, September 28, 1999

Bush critics charged that he was just a front for the moneymen who actually ran the team, an empty suit with p.r. skills.
–Eric Pooley, Time, June 21, 1999

"Being the President's son puts you in the limelight," he says. "While in the limelight, you might as well sell tickets...I like selling tickets."
–George W. Bush, Time, July 31, 1989

Bush became a Rangers managing partner, for which he was paid $200,000 a year. At once, the new owners told the city of Arlington they wanted a new stadium or they would move the team to another Texas city.
–Paul Alexander, Rolling Stone, August 5, 1999

Bush and the new owners, building a new stadium would be the first, and perhaps the most important, step to success...But the cost of such a park was estimated at $189 million, and even though they were among the richest men in Texas-and the United States-the new owners didn't want to pay for it.
—Byron York The American Spectator; June 1999

The cost of what became known as the Ballpark at Arlington was $191 million, out of which the owners would contribute $30 million, which would be raised through a loan and a "seat option bond" (a one-time fee that box-seat season-ticket holders would pay to keep their tickets). The other $161 million would be raised by implementing a half-cent sales tax in Arlington.
—Paul Alexander, Rolling Stone, August 5, 1999

Mr. Bush kept a low profile as his new baseball partners aggressively and successfully lobbied for a special referendum in which the voters of Arlington, Texas, approved a sales-tax increase to cover the $135 million cost of a new stadium. Texas conservatives denounced the measure as "corporate welfare."
—Micah Morrison, Wall Street Journal, September 28, 1999

With Bush's father in the White House, the Rangers did not want the politics of the new stadium to become partisan. Bush critics speculate that the aspiring politician also did not want to be closely associated with a tax increase.
—Kevin Sack, New York Times, May 9, 1999

A referendum was held in January 1991, and it was a smashing success for Bush and the Rangers. Voters turned out in record numbers to overwhelmingly approve the tax increase.
Byron York, The American Spectator, June 1999

In 1993, while walking around the stadium, Bush told a reporter from the Houston Chronicle, "When all those people in Austin say, `He ain't never done anything,' well, this is it."
—Robert Bryce, Texas Observer, January 16-22, 1998

"Am I going to benefit off it financially? I hope so," he told reporters.
–Byron York, The American Spectator, June 1999

Ordinary folks - most of whom probably have a hard time meeting their mortgage payments - dug into their pockets to make George W. a rich man.
–Robert Sherrill, Texas Monthly, July 1999

Last week, Bush and his partners hit what can only be described as a towering home run by selling the Texas Rangers to Thomas Hicks for $250 million. Bush, in particular, made a killing. For his 1.8% share of the club, which initially cost him $605,000, Hicks will pay the governor between $10 million and $14 million. That is return of up to 23 times Bush's original investment in less than nine years.
–Robert Bryce, Austin Chronicle, January 16-22, 1998

"I think when it is all said and done, I will have made more money than I ever dreamed I would make."
–Fort Worth Star-Telegram, January, 1998

What had made the ball club so valuable was a gift from the public - a $200 million stadium mostly paid for by a sales tax that the citizens of Arlington, Texas, had overwhelmingly voted to assume.
–Robert Sherrill, Texas Monthly, July 1999

I just want people when they say 'Texas Rangers' that they think here's a group of people trying to improve somebody's life.
–George W. Bush, United Press International, March 18, 1989

George W. Bush and the other owners of the Texas Rangers are deadbeats. Rich deadbeats, but deadbeats nevertheless...they still haven't paid the $7.5 million they owe the city of Arlington.
–Robert Bryce, Texas Observer, January 16-22, 1998

There are a lot of parallels between baseball and politics.
–George W. Bush, Time, July 31, 1989

People have certain expectations from the son of a president, particularly the oldest one.
—George W. Bush, Houston Chronicle, August 16, 1988

Until his 1994 election as governor of Texas, Dubya lived deep in his father's shadow. President Bush was an academic and athletic star at Andover and Yale, a war hero and successful oilman. George W. was an academic slacker at the same schools, a mediocre athlete, a member of the Texas Air National Guard during the Vietnam War and an unsuccessful oilman.
—Jonathan Alter, Newsweek, November 22, 1999

When George W. finally began breaking the news that he planned to run for governor against Ann Richards in 1994, many of his friends just laughed him off.
—Elizabeth Mitchell, "W: Revenge of the Bush Dynasty" (2000)

I vividly remember the night I first thought I might run for Governor. It was May 1, 1993.
—George W. Bush, "A Charge to Keep" (1999)

You can't be shaving one morning and look at yourself in the mirror and think, "I'm so pretty I'll run for Governor."
—Texas Governor Ann Richards, March 1994

Ms. Richards has already been diminishing her potential rival by referring to him as Shrub, as in a small bush, and Junior. He is not technically a Junior because he has only three of his father's four names. As Ms. Richards drily observed to advisers, "He's missing his Herbert."
—Maureen Dowd, New York Times, November 30, 1993

The test scores are up, the kids are looking better, the dropout rate is down. All of a sudden, you've got some jerk who's running for public office...and he's doesn't give your credit for doing your job."
—Texas Governor Ann Richards, Texarcana, TX, August 16, 1994

How did it feel, being called a jerk? I laughed it off.
—George W. Bush, "A Charge To Keep" (1999)

We're having a flappette here in Texas because Governor Ann Richards referred to her opponent, Shrub Bush, as "some jerk."..."Some jerk" does not rise to the level of even a small slight. Nevertheless, The New York Times thought it was a front-page story. Commentators waxed indignant. Texas Republicans, their notoriously delicate sensibilities wounded to the quick, swooned in shock. I don't know why Richards didn't just call him a peckerwood the way everyone else does.
—The Progressive, October 1994

If the tart-tongued eldest Bush son wins, he will have the satisfaction of running against the tart-tongued woman who mocked his father at the 1988 Democratic National Convention as a preppy with a silver foot in his mouth.
—Maureen Dowd, New York Times, November 30, 1993

Some who know the Bush family well believe Dubya ran against Richards at least in part out of a vindictive grudge stemming from her making fun of his daddy.
—Molly Ivins, Lou Dubose, "Shrub" (2000)

"All that I ask," he says, giving me another glare, "is that for once you guys stop seeing me as the son of George Bush. This campaign is about me, no one else."
—Texas Monthly, May 1994

"I don't need him to be elected governor," he says with a wave of his unlit cigar. The statement is intriguing primarily because of the speaker: George Walker Bush, eldest son of the president.
—Robert Tomsho, Wall Street Journal, April 3, 1989

"The only reason I'm talking to you," says George W., pointing his unlit cigar at me like a weapon, "is so people can know what I stand for, not so we can discuss family history. The minute the other George Bush wades into the process, my message gets totally obscured."
—Skip Hollandsworth, Texas Monthly, May 1994

Unqualified to govern Texas? No problem! The single most common misconception is that he has been running a large state for the past six years.
—Molly Ivins, Lou Dubose, "Shrub" (2000)

"My biggest liability in Texas," he says in his twang-free interview voice, "is the question, 'What's the boy ever done? So he's got a famous father and ran a small oil company. He could be riding on Daddy's name if he ran for office.'
—Laurence I. Barrett, Time, July, 31, 1989

George W. called his father every couple of weeks to talk during that campaign, but refused to acknowledge any dependence on him. When a reporter asked, "What do your parents think about you running?" He snapped, "I didn't ask their advice."
—Elizabeth Mitchell, "W: The Revenge of the Bush Dynasty" (2000)

People didn't vote for me when I was running for governor because I was George Bush's son...When people got into that voting booth they didn't say, "I think I'm going to vote for George W., because he was raised by George H. W."
—Howard Fineman, Jonathan Alter, Newsweek, January 24, 2000

The argument about whether he ever would have been elected to anything if his name weren't George W. Bush is pointless. His name is Bush...That W. Bush has traded on his father's name all his life is observably true. In fact, one could argue that he's never done anything else.
—Molly Ivins, Lou Dubose, "Shrub" (2000)

I think our country is ready for a fresh start after a season of cynicism.
—Gov. George W. Bush, Remarks at Bob Jones University, February 2, 2000

Bush's speech (at Bob Jones University) was intended to raise the enthusiasm of fundamentalist Christians in the state for his candidacy. He
delivered the standard stump speech he directs at religious conservatives
without acknowledging or criticizing the university's ban on racial dating
or the fact that school leaders view Catholicism as a cult.
—R.G. Ratcliffe, Houston Chronicle, March 7, 2000

By failing to condemn the school's denunciations of Catholicism and its ban on
interracial dating, he allowed McCain to create the impression that his compassionate words were at odds with his actions.
—Dana Milbank. The Washington Post, March 20, 2000

Self-described as a 'uniter, not a divider,' Bush has managed to
unite the Christian right, homophobes, zealous anti-abortion-
ists, the Rev. Pat Robertson, Ralph Reed, Strom Thurmond...if
this is compassionate conservatism, it's hard to imagine the
harsher kind.
—Richard Cohen, Denver Post, February 25, 2000

The governor himself doesn't think he'll have much trouble restoring his compassionate image. "I'm not worried about Bob Jones," he says in an interview. "I feel like I'm in good shape. It's me and my record. People will make up their own minds."
—Dana Milbank, The Washington Post, March 20, 2000

Three weeks after his Bob Jones appearance, Bush, mindful of the potential loss of Catholic voters, finally wrote a letter of apology to New York's Cardinal John O'Connor, apologizing not for his visit but for his failure to reproach the school for its contemptible anti-Catholicism.
—Cynthia Tucker, The Atlanta Constitution. March 1, 2000

I am offended by any suggestion that I tolerate anti-Catholic bigotry — and resent any attempt to create that impression. I hope that you, and all Catholics, will accept this assurance of my good faith.
—Letter from Gov. George W. Bush of Texas to Cardinal John O'Connor, February 25, 2000

The controversy is not over George W.'s intolerance; it's over his cowardice. Few believe the amiable Texas governor is a bigot; nothing in his legislative or personal history suggests that. But when he found himself down and out — thrashed by upstart Sen. John McCain in New Hampshire — he was not above consorting with bigots in an effort to regain a winning edge.
—Cynthia Tucker, The Atlanta Constitution, March 1, 2000

I take seriously my duty to encourage tolerance and respect for the religious views of others.
—Letter from Gov. George W. Bush of Texas to Cardinal John O'Connor, February 25, 2000

Faith is an important part of my life. I believe it is important to live my faith, not flaunt it.
—George W. Bush, "A Charge To Keep" (1999)

It's been generations since so many politicians have talked so much about Jesus—and their personal relationship with him. Just back from a jog, George W. Bush is game to talk more..."What are we talking about?" Faith. "Good. I like talking about faith."
—Franklin Foer, U.S. News & World Report, December 6, 1999

With a Bible in one hand and a cell phone—on which he speaks regularly to Christian Coalition leader turned political consultant Ralph Reed—in the other, Bush sounded more like a Southern minister than a presidential contender.
—Paul Alexander, Rolling Stone, August 5, 1999

Asked during the Iowa Republican presidential candidate debate "what political philosopher or thinker do you most identify with," George W. Bush shocked the journalistic, political and possibly some in the religious establishment when he unhesitatingly replied, "Christ, because he changed my heart."
—Los Angeles Times, December 18, 1999

Pressed to elaborate, the Texas governor again showed his inability to go deep....His mouth curled down into that famous smirky look. "Well, if they don't know, it's going to be hard to explain," he said. "When you turn your heart and your life over to Christ, when you accept Christ as the Savior, it changes your heart. It changes your life. And that's what happened to me." Translation: You're either in the Christ club or out of it, on the J.C. team or off.
—Maureen Dowd, New York Times, December 15, 1999

By cutting Christ to a sound bite, some said, he re-created exactly what he was trying to avoid: buying off evangelicals with a buzzword.
—Hanna Rosin, The Washington Post, December 16, 1999

I was asked what (philosopher most) influenced my life and I gave an honest, unvarnished answer.
—George W. Bush, GOP Debate, Durham, NC, January 6, 2000

Part of Bush's strategy is to woo religious voters with his choice of words and life story. He doesn't need to rail against abortion to convince evangelicals he's on their team.
—Franklin Foer, U.S. News & World Report, December 6, 1999

Bush's religious statements helped evangelicals feel more comfortable with him.
—Gustav Niebuhr, New York Times, February 21, 2000

The Rev. Jerry Falwell, who once led the Moral Majority, says he has informed his network of politically active pastors that Mr. Bush is his choice. Pat Robertson, founder of the Christian Coalition, is praising Mr. Bush at events. Ralph Reed, once the youthful face of the Christian Coalition, is now a consultant who counts Mr. Bush among his clients. "George W. would make an awesome president," Mr. Falwell said in an interview.
—Laurie Goodstein, New York Times, January 23, 2000

This is the era of niche marketing, and Jesus is a niche. Why not use the son of God to help the son of Bush appeal to voters? W. is checking Jesus' numbers, and Jesus is polling well in Iowa. Christ, the new wedge issue.
–Maureen Dowd, New York Times, December 15, 1999

He was supposed to steer clear of the scary Pat Robertson crowd. He was supposed to attract new voters to the GOP. Instead, when he found himself on the ropes, Bush ran for the smothering embrace of religious activists whose very agenda is to separate Americans into warring camps; dividing, not uniting.
–Cynthia Tucker, The Atlanta Constitution. March 1, 2000

We don't believe in tolerance in spite of our faith. We believe in tolerance because of our faith. And it leads us to condemn all forms of religious bigotry.
–George W. Bush, Remarks at the Simon Wiesenthal Center, March 6, 2000

As Texas governor and as a Republican candidate for president, Bush has had to write letters of apology and clarification to both the Anti-Defamation League, a Jewish watchdog group, and to Cardinal John O'Connor of New York. Bush created a minor stir last month in New York by confusing the Muslim religion with Louis Farrakhan's Nation of Islam.
–R.G. Ratcliffe, Houston Chronicle, March 7, 2000

This doesn't look good for Bush, who once got into trouble for doubting whether non-Christians could go to Heaven.
–Dana Milbank, The Washington Post, March 20, 2000

To a Jewish reporter, Bush recounted how shortly after he found renewed faith in Jesus Christ in the early 1980s he got into an argument with his mother over whether Jews could go to heaven because they do not believe in Jesus as their savior. Former first lady Barbara Bush got evangelist Billy Graham on the phone to tell Bush it was not his place to decide who goes to heaven.
–R.G. Ratcliffe, Houston Chronicle; March 7, 2000

Former first lady Barbara Bush said Sunday said that she was not surprised that her son, GOP presidential candidate George W. Bush, had invoked Jesus Christ in a recent debate, saying that the family views him as "our religious guru."
—Bennett Roth, Houston Chronicle, December 20, 1999

"I believe God decides who goes to heaven, not George W. Bush."
—George W. Bush, Houston Chronicle, March 7, 2000

Bush, a Methodist, reads daily from The One Year Bible; he prays with ministers on his cell phone; he asks staff, "Did you go to church on Sunday?"
—Franklin Foer, U.S. News & World Report, December 6, 1999

Religion to me is a very personal matter.
—George W. Bush, New York Times, January 23, 2000

CHAPTER SEVENTEEN:
Defend the Right to Free Choice

t is compassionate to offer practical help to women and children in
risis.
–Governor George W. Bush, Cedar Rapids, Iowa, June 12, 1999

will do everything in my power to restrict abortions.
–George W. Bush, The Dallas Morning News, October 22, 1994

Bush is "profoundly on the pro-life side...I'm not going to take issue with a few
words," said Pat Robertson, Founder of the Christian Coalition.
–San Francisco Chronicle, March 13, 1999

W. Bush is himself a born-again Christian who wants a constitutional
amendment outlawing abortion, although he seldom mentions that in
front of a general audience.
–Molly Ivins, Lou Dubose, "Shrub" (2000)

America is not ready to overturn Roe v. Wade because America's
hearts are not right.
–George W. Bush, The Associated Press, March 8, 1999

"Roe vs. Wade was a reach, overstepped the constitutional bounds as far as I'm
concerned," Bush told a news conference in his strongest anti-abortion comments so far in his presidential campaign.
–Houston Chronicle, January 23, 2000

Bush is not soft on abortion. He is a good pro-life candidate," Darla St.
Martin, Associate Director of the National Right to Life Committee.
–Washington Post, May 23, 1999

I think it's very important for the Republican Party to be viewed as the pro-life
party.
–George W. Bush, Austin American-Statesman, June 12, 1996

Some advocates of life will challenge why I oppose abortion yet support
the death penalty; to me, it's the difference between innocence and guilt.
–George W. Bush, "A Charge to Keep"

I personally believe there is life, and therefore take the position I take.
—George W. Bush, Associated Press, March 8, 1999

We must reduce the number of abortions in Texas and America by encouraging adoption, by promoting abstinence."
—George W. Bush, 1995 State of the State Address

And, you know, hopefully, condoms will work, but it hasn't worked.
—George W. Bush, Meet the Press, November 21, 1999

Gov. George W. Bush is disappointed that condoms are among the over-the-counter medical items that will be exempt from Texas sales taxes beginning next month, a spokeswoman says.
—Michael Holmes, Associated Press, March 22, 2000

Forcing Gov. George W. Bush to talk about abortion can be more challenging than getting a child to eat broccoli. He almost never raises the issue—or even utters the word—on his own. For months, he ignored his Republican rivals who assailed him relentlessly for his silence. Not until late last week...did Mr. Bush, cornered by reporters, offer more emphatic remarks about his opposition to abortion. He was squirming all the way.
—Richard L. Berke, New York Times, January 23, 2000

"I just know what I believe. I am pro-life," Bush said in Austin. "I've had a clear and consistent position ever since I got into politics."
—Houston Chronicle, March 23, 1999

Bush is walking a tightrope on the issue of abortion: he's publicly staking out a moderate pro-choice position while remaining personally "pro-life." And surprisingly, anti-abortion conservatives don't mind.
—Margaret Sykes, U.S. News & World Report, July 19, 1999

CHAPTER EIGHTEEN:
Justice Should Be Served With Compassion

We have zero-tolerance for troublemakers in the state of Texas.
—George W. Bush, Houston, TX, September 28, 1998

Bush is a firm believer in the death penalty. "I've always believed the death penalty will deter death," he said. "It'll save some victim"
—Law Street Journal, January 21, 1998

There must be a kindness in our justice. There must be a mercy in our judgment. There must be a love behind our zeal.
—George W. Bush, Indianapolis, Indiana, July 22, 1999

In his five years as governor, Mr. Bush has presided over the executions of 111 men and 1 woman, far more than any other governor in any other state since the Supreme Court in 1976 allowed reinstatement of the death penalty. Texas leads the nation in putting inmates to death; in 1997 it executed 4 inmates in one week, 8 in one month and 37 for the year, all modern records.
—Jim Yardley, New York Times, Jan 7, 2000

It is a fact that barbarism can appear even in the most outwardly civilized society.
—George W. Bush, Remarks at the Simon Wiesenthal Center, March 6, 2000

Bush's addiction to the death cult actually touches every important aspect of what could be described as his "politics."
—Christopher Hitchens, Salon, August 7, 1999

For Mr. Bush, the death penalty has helped define him as a politician. By any measure, his commitment to capital punishment is unquestioned.
—Jim Yardley, New York Times, January 7, 2000

Texas leads the United States by far in the execution of criminals; 162 inmates have died in the Huntsville death chamber since 1982. All Texas executions are carried out by lethal injection at Huntsville's prison. Residents take executions in stride. "It's like Detroit and making cars—it's what we do. No big deal," said John Strickland, owner of the Cafe Texan.
—Colin Nickerson, Boston Globe, November 25, 1998

Justice Should Be Served With Compassion

A Houston Chronicle poll released last week found that 71 percent of the adult Texans surveyed said that Bush's position on the (Karla Faye) Tucker case would have no impact on their decision about whether to vote for him.
—R.G. Ratcliffe, Houston Chronicle, February 4, 1998

Tucker had undergone a death row conversion to Christianity, married the prison chaplain and become a model inmate. Evangelical Christians seized on her story as proof of the transforming power of God, and religious leaders from Pat Robertson to Pope John Paul II called on the governor to grant clemency.
—Jim Yardley, New York Times, January 7, 2000

Had he commuted her sentence, he would have been faced with executing a black woman, Erica Sheppard, who was next in line on the female death row and had foregone her appeal. Spare a photogenic white girl and then kill a defiant black one? Better to do away with both and avoid the row altogether.
—Christopher Hitchens, Salon, August 7, 1999

Two days before the execution, one of his twin daughters told him at the dinner table "she had decided she opposes capital punishment." However, Mr. Bush said he chose not to intervene with a 30-day stay because of the precedent it would set.
—Wayne Slater, Dallas Morning News, November 16, 1999

At 6:12 p.m. Bush decided against granting a 30-day reprieve to Tucker, clearing the way for her execution in Huntsville 33 minutes later...In appealing for mercy, she said she wanted to live to continue a prison ministry.
—R.G. Ratcliffe, Houston Chronicle, February 4, 1998

I would like to say to all of you—the Thornton family and Jerry Dear's family that I am so sorry. I hope God will give you peace with this. Baby, I love you. Ron, give Peggy a hug for me. Everybody has been so good to me. I love all of you very much. I am going to be face to face with Jesus now...You have been so good to me. I love all of you very much. I will see you all when you get there. I will wait for you.
—Last Statement of Karla Faye Tucker

May God bless Karla Faye Tucker.
—George W. Bush, Houston Chronicle, February 4, 1998

A much-remarked Talk magazine article described Mr. Bush as "smirk-ing" in an interview when he recalled the unsuccessful efforts of killer-turned-Christian Karla Faye Tucker and her supporters to stay her execu-tion.
—Jackie Calmes, Wall Street Journal, December 3, 1999

Bush is portrayed in Talk magazine as ridiculing pickax killer Karla Faye Tucker of Houston for an interview she did with CNN broadcaster Larry King shortly before she was executed last year.
—Houston Chronicle, August 11, 1999

"Please," Bush whimpers, his lips pursed in mock desperation, "don't kill me."
—Talk, September 1999

'I think it is nothing short of unbelievable that the governor of a major state running for president thought it was acceptable to mock a woman he decided to put to death," (Gary) Bauer said of Bush. "If you are going to call yourself a compassionate conservative, you might want to look up the meaning of compassion."
–Houston Chronicle, August 11, 1999

He actually seemed to bear the dead woman a grudge for the political headaches she had caused him.
–Marjorie Williams, The Washington Post, January 7, 2000

On the death penalty, he laughs about it; he's so sure of himself, even though five of his fellow Governors are so disturbed by new evidence that convictions were brought about by faulty forensics, coerced confessions and false accusations that they've placed a moratorium on executions. Yet Bush insists he hasn't made and couldn't make a mistake.
–Margaret Carlson, Time, March 20, 2000

"All I can tell you," Mr. Bush said in 1998, " is that for the four years I've been governor, I am confident we have not executed an innocent person, and I'm confident that the system has worked to make sure there is full access to the courts."
–Jim Yardley, New York Times, January 7, 2000

Minorities were receiving a grossly disproportionate share of those sentences. That was nowhere truer than in Texas, according to the authors of "The Rope, the Chair & the Needle," a statistical analysis of capital punishment here, published in 1994.
–Paul Duggan, The Washington Post, December 9, 1998

Once you have a death penalty statute, it must be applied fairly.
–George W. Bush, "A Charge to Keep" (1999)

Gov. George Bush on the execution of Mario Marquez, a mentally retarded man with the mental capacity of a 7 year old: "If we want our young Texans to learn to make correct choices, the consequences of bad behavior must be certain and must be clear."
—Village Voice, February 21, 1995

I have nothing against pardoning. I just haven't been very aggressive on it.
—George Bush, Larry King Live, February 2, 2000

Emile Duhamel, a mentally ill and retarded man on death row, died on July 9 from the heat. He was taking prescription drugs that made him extra-sensitive to heat. Guards had taken away his eight-inch fan. Yet according to prison officials, he died of natural causes. He was cremated the next day before his family was notified.
—Gloria Rubac, Workers World News Service, August 20, 1998

In Texas we love you a lot, but there will be bad consequences for bad behavior.
—George W. Bush, Houston, TX, September 28, 1998

Critics describe the Texas system for capital crimes as the most unfair and merciless of the 38 states with a death penalty, saying it deprives the accused of adequate legal aid and appeals. But other states, including Florida, where Mr. Bush's brother Jeb is governor, see Texas as a model of efficiency.
—Jim Yardley, New York Times, January 7, 2000

Is compassion beneath us? Is mercy below us? Should our party be led by someone who boasts a hard heart?
—George W. Bush, CNN, June 12, 1999

Joseph Stanley Faulder on Thursday became the first Canadian in almost a half-century to be executed in the United States. Faulder, 61, was pronounced dead at 6:18 p.m., six minutes after the flow of lethal drugs began. He coughed twice, let out two gasps and then stopped moving.
—Michael Graczyk, Houston Chronicle, June 18, 1999

His case created a controversy in Canada...Canada doesn't have the death penalty, presumably because many—if not most—Canadians oppose it.
—Clay Robinson, Houston Chronicle, December 13, 1998

Canadian authorities say (Faulder) should be spared because he was not granted consular rights when he was arrested by Texas police.
—Paul Duggan, The Washington Post, December 9, 1998

Bush said he wouldn't let the criticism affect his decision. "No one is going to threaten the governor of the state of Texas," he said during an appearance in San Antonio.
—Renae Merle, Jim Henderson, Houston Chronicle, December 8, 1998

The Canadian reporter asked Bush what he would say to Canadians "who seem to think that your state is running kind of a Wild West show down here." "If you're a Canadian and you come to our state, don't murder anybody," Bush replied.
—Clay Robinson, Houston Chronicle, December 13, 1998

The history of our great state of Texas is written with the blood of people who never gave up and never gave in.
—George W. Bush, Mission High School Graduation, Mission, TX, May 29, 1998

As for the possibility of a reprieve from the governor for Faulder, Bush said: "We're a death penalty state. We believe in swift and sure punishment."
—Associated Press, December 10, 1998

I have concluded judgments about the heart and soul of an individual on death row are best left to a higher authority.
—George W. Bush, Houston Chronicle, February 4, 1998

I support tough laws and long sentences for those who use guns to commit crimes.
—George W. Bush, Associated Press, February 6, 2000

George W. Bush on Sep 1, 1994 shot and killed a killdeer, a protected songbird which he had mistaken for a dove while hunting. Bush was fined $130.
—U.S. News & World Report; October 17, 1994

After tramping across a cornfield, Bush sighted his prey, leveled his shotgun and fired, nearly obliterating his catch. Upon inspection of the remains, however, the soon-to-be governor made a troubling discovery. He'd downed a killdeer, which, as any novice bird watcher knows, looks nothing like a dove—or any other game bird, for that matter. Indeed, in Texas the killdeer is listed as a threatened species.
—Jeffrey St. Clair, In These Times, March 6, 2000

Democratic opponent Ann W. Richards wasted no time in ridiculing Bush, suggesting that a real Texan would never have committed such a gaffe. "You can't get dressed up in a hunting jacket, borrow somebody's shotgun and head out into the field. You just can't do it. You'll kill the wrong bird ever' time."
—U.S. News & World Report, October 17, 1994

"It was a humiliating experience," Bush said Thursday while discussing his plans to go hunting on Sunday, a year after the killdee killing. It was, he said, "the highest fine I've ever paid."
—Houston Chronicle, September 31, 1995

In the end, it did not hurt, and it may have helped.
—George W. Bush, "A Charge to Keep" (1999)

This act of savagery actually may have won him a few votes.
—Jeffrey St. Clair, In These Times, March 6, 2000

He is governor today because of guns.
—Ann Richards, Lou Dubose, "Shrub" (2000)

Guns are an issue in Texas, as they are in America.
—George W. Bush, "A Charge to Keep" (1999)

Bush promised gun enthusiasts that he would sign a bill ending the state's century-old ban on the carrying of sidearms by civilians—and he did. Now, to the dismay of gun control advocates, more than 200,000 Texans are licensed to carry concealed handguns, and the number continues to go up.
—Paul Duggan, The Washington Post, March 16, 2000

Ignoring a plea by the Humane Society of the United States, Texas Gov. George W. Bush has accepted a conservation award from an organization of trophy hunters that the society says promotes the killing of rare species.
—Martin Griffith, Associated Press, February 6, 2000

The killdeer incident helped fill in blanks the voters may have had about what type of person I was.
—George W. Bush, "A Charge to Keep" (1999)

There is no telling when I might go hunting again.
—George W. Bush, State of the State Address, Austin, TX, February 7, 1995

"Sometimes the idea of compassion is dismissed as soft or sentimental...Compassion is not one of the easy virtues."
—George W. Bush, Indianapolis, Indiana, July 22, 1999

When a woman in Florence, S.C., asked him what to do about her medical insurance not covering all the needs of her seriously ill son, he was stumped. "I'm sorry," he answered. "I wish I could wave a wand."
—Maureen Dowd, New York Times, February 22, 2000

It is compassionate to make sure nobody gets left behind.
—Governor George W. Bush, June 1999

Bush startled anti-hunger activists this weekend when he doubted that anyone in his state lacked adequate food. Bush told the Fort Worth Star-Telegram, "I'd like to know who's going hungry in the state of Texas." When Bush heard that hunger was widespread in his own state, he sounded incredulous. "You'd think the governor would have heard if there are pockets of hunger in Texas," Bush said.
—Associated Press, December 21, 1999

Among Texans ages 19 to 65, the percentage without (health) coverage rose slightly under Mr. Bush and is higher than in any state but Arizona. The numbers are even worse among poor children, and hundreds of thousands of them are not enrolled in Medicaid, even though they qualify.
—New York Times, April 11, 2000

Yet all around this country, I have argued that prosperity must have a higher purpose. The purpose of prosperity is to make sure the American dream touches every willing heart. The purpose of prosperity is to leave no one out.
—George W. Bush, Latin Business Association Luncheon, September 2, 1999

Since Bush became governor in 1995, Texas has consistently been first in its vast population of the uninsured. It is sometimes first, sometimes second in uninsured kids, but consistently first among women....Texas is third in the incidence of hunger.
—Thomas Oliphant, Boston Globe, November 16, 1999

I believe in these principles. I have seen them turn around troubled schools in my state. I've seen them bring hope into the lives of children—inspiring confidence and ambition.
—George W. Bush, Little Rock, Arkansas, March 24, 2000

Skeptics suggest the Texas test scores have been inflated by intensive test drills, the selective exemption of disadvantaged students from the test — and even cheating by schools and districts that want to improve their images. Such a conclusion does not sit well with Bush, who has made education a centerpiece of his quest for the White House.
—Baltimore Sun, March 28, 2000

School districts must be encouraged, not mandated, to start "Tough Love Academies." These alternative schools would be staffed by a different type of teacher, perhaps retired Marine drill sergeants, who understand that discipline and love go hand-in-hand."
—George W. Bush, State of the State Address, Austin, TX, February 7, 1995

Ironically, one of the most telling aspects of Bush's tenure as governor is that, for all his talk of compassion, he has been most consistently stingy on policies affecting children. In 1999 he vigorously supported voucher legislation that would have allowed children from 80 public school systems in Texas's six largest metropolitan areas to opt out of the public school system with taxpayerbacked tuition credits....

Even more troubling was the governor's decision to try to block coverage for 200,000 children under the federally funded Children's Health Insurance Program (CHIP).

—Robert Dreyfuss, The American Prospect, Sept/Oct 1999

A president does not bear responsibility for every policy in every school in every district. But a president must be the keeper of our common ideals. A president speaks for everyone.

—George W. Bush, Little Rock, Arkansas, March 24, 2000

A partially blind biology student said she couldn't afford a $400 device that would let her use a microscope, his solution was to ask if anyone in the audience would pay for it. Noblesse oblige is not exactly a detailed health care program.

—Maureen Dowd, New York Times, February 22, 2000

A president—and sometimes only a president—can speak for the common good.

—George W. Bush, Little Rock, AK, March 24, 2000

The compassion proclaimed to be so widespread in George W Bush's Texas may look to the rest of us like official indifference and cruelty.

—Thomas Oliphant, Boston Globe, November 16, 1999

Help The Less Fortunate

I wish I knew the law that would cause people to love each other. I do not.
—Governor George W. Bush, Inaugural Address, Austin, TX, January 17, 1995

Bush's state, meanwhile, has the highest percentage of women without health insurance, according to one private health group, and four in 10 women over 50 haven't had a mammogram in two years.
—Maureen Dowd, New York Times, February 22, 2000

My compassionate conservatism philosophy is making Texas a better place. But today's election says something more. It says that a leader who is compassionate and conservative can erase the gender gap, open the doors of the Republican Party to new faces and new voices, and win without sacrificing our principles.
—George W. Bush, Victory Speech, Austin, TX; November 3, 1998

His compassionate conservative thing....is absolutely brilliant...George W. is running as a Third Way Republican. And compassionate conservative captures that perfectly. Also, there's no good equivalent for our side. The best I can do is heartless liberal.
---Al Franken George, October 1999

Tolerance can never be assumed. It must always be taught.
—George W. Bush, Simon Wiesenthal Center, March 6, 2000

Republican presidential candidate George W. Bush sharply told a black voter to "sit down" after the man questioned him about his stance on the Confederate flag flying over the South Carolina Capitol.
—R.G. Ratcliffe, Houston Chronicle, February 16, 2000

A leader must do more than hold this conviction. He must give it voice. And he must give it force.
—George W. Bush, Simon Wiesenthal Center, March 6, 2000

George W. refrained from traveling to Jasper, Texas, after James Byrd Jr., a black man, was decapitated after being dragged to his death by several white men...critics chastised him for not taking the occasion to make stronger statements about race issues.
—Elizabeth Mitchell, "W: Revenge of the Bush Dynasty" (2000)

Charming pictures (show) him cuddling little brown kids and reading to little black kids...what's a lot harder to find is any evidence that he's done anything at all as governor of Texas that would make any difference in their lives, except to make them harder.
—Molly Ivins, Lou Dubose, "Shrub" (2000)

The teaching of our tradition is simple and permanent: "Love your neighbor as yourself."
—George W. Bush, Simon Wiesenthal Center, March 6, 2000

It is far more compassionate to turn away people at the border than to attempt to find and arrest them once they are living in our country illegally.
—George W. Bush, "A Charge to Keep" (1999)

Its Mexican border is a hotbed of contagion. The state ranks near the top in the nation in rates of AIDS, diabetes, tuberculosis and teenage pregnancy, and near the bottom in immunizations, mammograms and access to physicians. But since George W. Bush became governor in 1995, he has not made health a priority, his aides acknowledge. He has never made a speech on the subject, his press office says.
—New York Times, April 11, 2000

We must teach our children to respect people from all walks of life.
—George W. Bush, Simon Wiesenthal Center, March 6, 2000

Mr. Bush told a group of Christian conservatives "he would not 'know-ingly' appoint a practicing homosexual as an ambassador or department head, but neither would he dismiss anyone who was discovered to be a homosexual after being named to a position." Gee, how compassionate can you get?
—Frank Rich, New York Times, April 8, 2000

We must teach our children...that we are one nation, one people, all American.
—George W. Bush, Simon Wiesenthal Center, March 6, 2000

He supported a bill to make it illegal for gays or lesbians to adopt children or serve as foster parents. A particularly nasty feature of that bill was its failure to protect people who had adopted a child in the past and since come out as gay or lesbian; the state could take the child back.
—Molly Ivins, Lou Dubose, "Shrub" (2000)

This is the proper way to treat human beings created in the image and likeness of God. Many Americans, of many backgrounds, share the same conviction.
—George W. Bush, Simon Wiesenthal Center, March 6, 2000

When somebody makes it my business, like on gay marriage, I'm going to stand up and say I don't support gay marriage.
—George W. Bush, GOP Debate on Larry King Live, February 15, 2000

I believe our nation is chosen by God and commissioned by history to be a model to the world.
—George W. Bush, Simon Wiesenthal Center, March 6, 2000

There is a brashness, an honest directness in Texans that is sometimes viewed as too direct.
—George W. Bush, "A Charge to Keep" (1999)

Junior was the Roman candle of the family, bright, hot, a sparkler—and likeliest to burn the fingers. He had all the old man's high spirits, but none of his taste for accommodation.
—Richard Ben Cramer, "What It Takes" (1992)

The young Bush threw his weight around as necessary, serving as "loyalty thermometer" and blunt instrument, coming down hard on leakers, loose cannons and snarky reporters, mediating staff disputes from a generic office, where he chewed an unlighted cigar and spat bits of tobacco leaf in the general direction of a foam coffee cup.
—Eric Pooley, Time, June 21, 1999

Republican adviser Roger Stone says that "G.W. didn't have a title, but he was listened to because he was the candidate's son. He was a hothead with a very short fuse who was always looking for a fight, but ultimately G.W. and Atwater got along well." Following the election, which ended in Bush's victory over Michael Dukakis, George W. stayed on in Washington "long enough," Stone says, "to make sure the people who were for Bush got rewarded and the people who were against him got fucked."
—Paul Alexander, Rolling Stone, August 5, 1999

"Why you? Give me one reason why I should let you talk with George Bush?" It was the first question I asked, every time. I earned and deserved a reputation for being feisty and tough.
—George W. Bush, "A Charge to Keep" (1999)

The writers called him arrogant. "Just doing my job," George W. would reply, "protecting the old man."
—Skip Hollandsworth, Texas Monthly, May 1994

George W. Bush had method—hard to see, sometimes, but...method. He'd have a rotating gaggle in his office all day, bullshitting, playing with the toys on his

desk, giggling at the T-shirts and gimcracks tacked all over the walls, while Junior sat with his boots on the desk, a chew in his bottom lip, talkin' on the phone and spittin' in the basket...and listening. Sometimes people would get so easy in his office, they'd say what they thought. That's how Junior knew—what they said and what they thought.
—Richard Ben Cramer, "What It Takes" (1992)

He was an edgy, ominous presence from Texas, rocking on his boot heels, or standing off to the side of his father and glaring with a half-cocked grin at someone pressing his father on the adultery question, the wimp question, the gilded-upbringing question...sometimes he would mutter 'no comment, asshole.'"
—Bill Minutaglio, "First Son: George W. Bush and the Bush Family Dynasty" (1999)

The 1987 Newsweek cover with the headline "Fighting the Wimp Factor" was a searing experience for Vice President Bush, a war hero, and his hyper-loyal son. The story said many Republicans were worried that Mr. Bush might not be "strong enough or tough enough for the challenges of the Oval Office." W., still a hothead in those days, called the magazine's White House correspondent to inform him: "Newsweek's been cut off. You're out of business." In September 1988, the vice president was still so peeved that Katharine Graham, the publisher of Newsweek, had to meet with him to appease him. He had even counted the number of times the word "wimp" had been used in the story.
—Maureen Dowd, New York Times, February 16, 2000

My blood pressure still goes up when I remember the cover of Newsweek.
—George W. Bush, "A Charge to Keep" (1999)

His reputation in Washington, the way he was described on Capitol Hill, also grew. One writer would paint him as the 'Roman candle' in the Bush camp—sparkling and riveting but sometimes too hot to touch. But another writer said he was more like Sonny Corleone out doing some manly defense to retain respect to his father.
—Bill Minutaglio, "First Son: George W. Bush and the Bush Family Dynasty" (1999)

I had no formal role or title; I didn't need one...I was a loyalty enforcer.
—George W. Bush, "A Charge to Keep" (1999)

As George W. was leaving the restaurant, he approached (journalist Al) Hunt. "You fucking son of a bitch," he spewed at him. "I won't forget what you said, and you're going to pay a fucking price for it."
—Elizabeth Mitchell, "W: Revenge of the Bush Dynasty" (2000)

Hunt was dining with his wife, Judy Woodruff, and their 4-year- old son.
—George Lardner Jr, Lois Romano, The Washington Post, July 25, 1999

After Bush left Hunt and his family alone, a thought blinked in Hunt's head: "This is a guy who's got problems."
—Bill Minutaglio, "First Son: George W. Bush and the Bush Family Dynasty" (1999)

When the queen of England came to the United States and had dinner with the Bush family, Barbara seated George W. at the other end of the table so he wouldn't be heard saying anything offensive. "He's the Bush black sheep," she proudly told the queen.
—Skip Hollandsworth, Texas Monthly, May 1994

When the Bush campaign needed a tough-guy spokesman, George W. was trotted out. It was he, for example, who met with reporters to deny charges that his father had had an affair with longtime Bush staffer Jennifer Fitzgerald, a rumor that had become so widespread that the Washington Post once described Fitzgerald as a government worker "who has served president-elect Bush in a variety of positions," to the great hilarity of the Beltway crowd. The line George W. gave to reporters that day would become infamous: "The answer to the Big A question," he said, "is N-O."
—Paul Alexander, Rolling Stone, August 5, 1999

"We have a saying in our family," Junior said. "If a grenade is rolling by The Man, you dive on it first."
—George W. Bush, "Quest For the Presidency 1992" (1994)

One question being asked...is whether George W. Bush, the president's oldest son, is becoming the Nancy Reagan of the Bush White House. Put another way: Is the younger George Bush the member of the First Family with the most political clout?
—Gilbert A. Lewthwaite, Baltimore Sun December 15, 1991

You've got to ask the question, is the air cleaner since I became governor? And the answer is yes.
–George W. Bush, May 1999

By no known standard has the air of Texas improved under Governor Bush, nor has anything else involving the environment.
–Molly Ivins, Lou Dubose, "Shrub" (2000)

As we use nature's gifts, we must do so wisely.
–George W. Bush, April 2, 2000

Over nine million Texans—almost half of the state's population—reside in areas that do not meet federal standards for ozone levels.
–New York Times, November 9, 1999

Every environmental issue confronts us with a duty to be good stewards.
George W. Bush, April 2, 2000

His first appointment to the state's environmental protection agency, the Texas Natural Resources Conservation Commission, was Ralph Marquez, an executive who had spent 30 years with the Monsanto Chemical Company.
—Bob Herbert, New York Times, April 6, 2000

Texas ranked ahead of all states in the discharge of recognized carcinogens into the air.
—New York Times, April 6, 2000

"The air situation in Texas in January 1995 was fair to poor. But our state government has made it worse in the last five years," said Meg Haenn of the Texas Air Crisis Campaign. "We believe the air crisis is due to the intentional acts and conscious indifference of Governor Bush."
—Wayne Slater, Dallas Morning News, October 20, 1999

Asked if it had been a mistake for the Legislature to scuttle auto emissions testing in 1995—his first year in office—and whether his new push for cleaner fuels and cleaner—burning vehicles were too little, too late, Bush said, "No."
—Kathy Walt, Houston Chronicle, December 18, 1999

Houston this year has suffered 44 days of ozone levels that exceeded national health standards (one more than Los Angeles) and handily registered the highest ozone reading in the nation.
—David Whitman, Robert Bryce, U.S. News & World Report, Octob er 25, 1999

Mr. Bush's relationship to the environment is roughly that of a doctor to a patient—when the doctor's name is Kevorkian...(Texas) leads the nation in the number of factories violating clean-water standards. It leads the nation in the injection of toxic waste into underground wells.
—Bob Herbert, New York Times, April 6, 2000

At least nine members of Bush's "Pioneer" program—those donors pledged to raise $100,000 for Bush's campaign—are affiliated with polluting companies.
—New York Times, November 9, 1999

Bush got $169,400 from polluters in the first 28 days of his presidential fund-raising, plus $138,900 from lawyers with Vinson & Elkins. The law firm's clients include Aluminum Co. of America, whose Rockdale plant is the grandfathered site with the state's top air emissions.
—R.G. Ratcliffe, Houston Chronicle, May 1, 1999

Prosperity will mean little if we leave future generations a world of polluted air, toxic lakes and rivers.
—George W. Bush, April 2, 2000

That people-winning smile of Gov. George W. Bush's may have turned over-night into one of his biggest enemies, now known as The Smirk.
—R.G. Ratcliffe, Houston Chronicle. December 8, 1999

Smirk or smile, Texas Gov. [George W.] Bush's version of read my lips is start-ing to draw attention.
—Jackie Calmes, Wall Street Journal, December 3, 1999

Suddenly the pursed-lipped smile that crosses Bush's face in times of mirth and stress has become fodder for talk radio and a symbol of the larger question of whether Bush is a man of substance or an overgrown fraternity boy.
—R.G. Ratcliffe, Houston Chronicle, December 8, 1999

The Smirk can make one look like a jerk...It pops out indiscriminately—in times of peril as well as moments of mirth. It gives bystanders the sense they're deal-ing with an exhibi-tionistic frat boy who has poked a hole in the bottom of a beer can and wants an audience to watch him pop the top.
—Tony Snow, Denver Post, No-vember 14, 1999

To his critics, the look is one of a smug, late-blooming baby boomer who doesn't take anything seri-ously. To old friends in Texas, it's simply an endearing trait.
—Jackie Calmes, Wall Street Journal, December 3, 1999

George W. takes pride in his own irreverence. He loves to needle his friends.
—Skip Hollandsworth, Texas Monthly, May 1994

**His interview smirk—that anti-intellectual bravado—was jarring. Has he grown so accustomed to getting things easily—Yale, the National Guard, lucrative business deals—that he expects family connections to carry him through here?
—Maureen Dowd, The New York Times, November 7, 1999**

I have always looked for the lighter side of life.
—George W. Bush, "A Charge to Keep" (1999)

**Bush winks at folks a lot. A wink is kind of an intimate gesture, suggesting some special connection between the winker and the winkee...But winking can lose some of its intimacy if the winker is too promiscuous with the winks, and after observing George W. for a couple of days I'd say there's some danger of that.
—Al Franken, George, October 1999**

What lurks behind that smirk? That is the question that puzzles the political world as Republican presidential front-runner George W. Bush faces the nation with a perpetual half-grin.
—Jackie Calmes, Wall Street Journal, December 3, 1999

**When he forms his trademark smirk, a sort of half-grin that pushes the corners of his mouth straight up, he resembles a cocky college kid. It doesn't take much, however, for his smirk to turn into a sneer.
—Skip Hollandsworth, Texas Monthly, May 1994**

Like [Richard] Nixon's televised sweat, the smirk has come to represent in certain minds all that is wrong and potentially disqualifying about [George W.] Bush's ambitions. Just as Nixon's excruciatingly public perspiration allegedly revealed his discomfort in going head to head with a cool, dry and casual John F. Kennedy, Bush's smirk often is mentioned as proof that he's a lightweight playboy, a smugly superior smart-aleck who might use the presidential limo to pop wheelies.
—Chicago Tribune, February 15, 2000

As he sat at a table with two female workers there, he continuously wore a sort of smile as he listened to each woman. One of the women, a counselor for "post-abortion trauma," told how she had become pregnant at 20, helplessly felt she had no alternative but abortion," and for 15 years . . . suffered in silence." Still, the right side of Mr. Bush's mouth seemed frozen in a half smile.
—Jackie Calmes, Wall Street Journal, December 3, 1999

Bush's early appearances were complicated by what his friends described as a smile but what others saw as a smirk. Since then, the smirk seems to have been surgically removed....These days he frowns, smiles, laughs and even scowls, but he does not normally smirk - although occasionally he forgets himself when he is in a good mood and it creeps back, only to be replaced by a frown as soon as he notices it.
—Times-Picayune. March 5, 2000

I like to joke that a compassionate conservative is a conservative with a smile, not a conservative with a frown.
—George W. Bush, "A Charge to Keep" (1999)

I don't make any apologies for what I do on the campaign trail.
—George W. Bush, New York Times, February 24, 2000

Three weeks after his Bob Jones appearance, Bush, mindful of the potential loss of Catholic voters, finally wrote a letter of apology to New York's Cardinal John O'Connor, apologizing not for his visit but for his failure to reproach the school for its contemptible anti-Catholicism.
—Cynthia Tucker, The Atlanta Constitution. March 1, 2000

Compassionate conservatism is neither soft or fuzzy. It is clear and compelling.
—George W. Bush, "A Charge to Keep" (1999)

Bush told an Iowa audience during Monday's Republican presidential debate that Christ was his favorite political philosopher, "because he changed my heart."
—Associated Press, December 14, 1999

Bush backed off his answer yesterday, telling an Iowa reporter he hadn't quite understood the question.
—Hanna Rosin, Washington Post; December 16, 1999

If you are weary of polls and posturing, of scandals and alibis, come join us.
—George W. Bush, Iowa Caucus Night, January 24, 2000

George W. Bush's nonstop battle with his own party's major gay organization makes a self-styled "compassionate conservative" and "uniter not a divider" increasingly look like a hypocrite.
—Frank Rich, New York Times, April 8, 2000

"All that does is create kind of a huge political nightmare for people," Mr. Bush said when asked whether he would meet with members of the Log Cabin Republicans.
—Wayne Slater, Dallas Morning News, November 22, 1999

Bush said he is likely to meet in coming days with members of the Log Cabin Republicans.
—Associated Press, April 8, 2000

Americans look at Washington and they don't like what they see. Who can blame them? They see...some who would rather score a point for the next election that get something done for the good of the nation.
—George W. Bush, "A Charge to Keep" (1999)

Too often, on social issues, my party has painted an image of America slouching toward Gemorrah.
—George Bush, New York Times, October 6, 1999

Bush has written a "private" letter of apology to Bork, which he said describes himself as "a fan" of the judge."
—Robert Novak, Creators Syndicate, October 14, 1999

George W. has to weasel: he has to convince the conservative minority that he's really on their side and will backtrack on his moderate statements when he gets into office, and he has to convince the moderate majority that he'll stab his religious allies in the back and hold to the positions he's been publicly espousing.
—Margaret Sykes, U.S. News & World Report, July 19, 1999

There ought to be limits to freedom.
—George W. Bush, Press Conference, May 21, 1999

Bush has shown a preoccupation with the Internet's potential to harm him.
—Terry M. Neal, Washington Post, November 30, 1999

Hackers apparently vandalized the campaign Web site for presidential candidate George W. Bush early Tuesday, replacing his photo with an image of a hammer and sickle and calling for "a new October revolution."
—Associated Press, May 20, 1999

Staffers have bought up some 60 domain names, including Bushsucks.com, Bushbites.com and Bushblows.com, to keep them out of the hands of pranksters.
—Martha Brant, Newsweek, September 20, 1999

An altered, obviously fake image appears of a gleeful-looking Texas Gov. George W. Bush with a straw up his nose, inhaling white lines. **Www.gwbush.com** is not, needless to say, the official Bush campaign Web site..and that's exactly the point, says the site's creator, Zack Exley, 29, a computer programmer from Boston.

—Terry M. Neal, Washington Post, November 30, 1999

"I figured Bush would be annoyed, and it would be fun to haggle with his campaign," says Exley.
—Martha Brant, Newsweek, September 20, 1999

Bush responded harshly to the site, which ribs the candidate for draft dodging and his alleged coke connoisseur days. At a May 21 press conference in Austin, Bush dismissed Exley as "a garbage man" and said "there ought to be limits to freedom."
—Donna Ladd, Village Voice, December 29, 1999

The Bush campaign also filed a complaint with the Federal Election Commission, accusing Exley of violating election laws and demanding he operate under the rules of a political committee.
—Terry M. Neal, Washington Post, November 30, 1999

Intolerance is not merely a problem of the past....Hate groups recruit on the Internet and warp the souls of children. We are called by conscience to set our hearts against all assaults on human dignity.
—George W. Bush, Simon Wiesenthal Center, March 6, 2000

Bush blamed popular culture for 'romanticizing violence.' He said he favored parental filtering devices for television and the Internet.
—Reuters, April 21, 1999

In February, months before Bush announced his candidacy, his top political adviser, Karl Rove, registered dozens of potentially off-color or pejorative domain names—at $70 a pop—so no one could use them to create Web sites that parody Bush.
—Terry M. Neal, Washington Post, November 30, 1999

Will the highways on the Internet become more few?
—George W. Bush, Concord, New Hampshire, January, 2000

We are conservatives because we believe in freedom.
—Governor George W. Bush, Bob Jones University, February

Every political campaign—every political victory—is empty unless it is used for some great purpose.
—George W. Bush's, Bob Jones University in South Carolina, February 2, 2000

Bush is something quite rare in today's presidential politics: a front-runner who has become the darling of his party's establishment even though most voters don't know much about who he is or what he stands for.
—Kenneth T. Walsh, U.S. News & World Report; June 7, 1999

Just as the senior Bush was perplexed by demands that he articulate a vision—give us a reason for him to be president—so his son seems stymied on the same grounds.
—Richard Cohen, The Washington Post, February 25, 2000

George Bush fighting the wimp factor? That rings a bell.
—Maureen Dowd, New York Times, February 16, 2000

The shadows of his father's successes are never far from George W. What ultimately doomed George Sr.'s presidency was the perception that he had no vision for America and that he broke his promise not to raise taxes. Now comes the son, a man who wants to be president because it will bring him not just more power and prestige but also personal vindication.
—Texas Monthly, June 1999

The Bush boys, who learned fanatic competition in sports and life from their father and grandmother, are driven by their desire to avenge Poppy's loss to Slick. Sometimes I think George W. wants to run just to put back the horseshoe pit that President Clinton covered over with a picnic area.
—Maureen Dowd, New York Times, November 4, 1998

How did a man who was, as a cousin once described it, "on the road to nowhere at age 40" find the road that led him here? Even some close friends are surprised by Bush's sudden rise. Others who knew him casually years ago are astonished that he might be deemed presidential timber.
—Eric Pooley, Time, June 21, 1999

His entire life has been the pursuit of accommodating himself to power—to his father, to his father's wealthy and influential friends, and, in his current incarnation as politician, to the Democratic leaders who controlled the Texas state legislature. In the end, what Bush really seems to stand for is business as usual.
—Paul Alexander, Rolling Stone, August 5, 1999

This may come as quite a shock to people, but I've never taken a poll or run a focus group to figure out what's the right public policy.
—George W. Bush, Houston, TX, September 28, 1998

In June 1997, the Zogby American poll came out with a report that 21 percent of the Republicans surveyed supported Bush as their 2000 presidential nominee...Bush's lead in the June 1997 poll was the first indication...he could be a serious presidential contender.
—R.G. Ratcliffe, Houston Chronicle, July 18, 1999

I feel as if I've already lived through the overstuffed Bush Rolodex and all those fund-raising receptions thrown by hostesses named Muffie and Buffie where the only hors d'oeuvres are a slim wedge of brie and a wilted clump of grapes. It's deja vu all over again
—Maureen Dowd, New York Times, November 4, 1998

Former President Bush is having a significant impact on his son's bid for the Republican presidential nomination even though he is rarely seen in the campaign and is almost never discussed on the stump.
—R.G. Ratcliffe, Houston Chronicle December 10, 1999

W.'s campaign has imitated his dad's playbook, which may be sorely out of date: pandering to the religious right, splashing mud on foes while promising to inspire Americans' "better angels."
—Maureen Dowd, New York Times, February 16, 2000

If you are tired of the bitterness that poisons our politics, come join us.
—George W. Bush, Iowa Caucus Night, January 24, 2000

Reminded of how McCain had boosted turnout in the primaries, Bush snapped, "Well, then, how come he didn't win?" Asked whether he had any second thoughts about his tactics, Bush replied, "Like what? Give me an example. What should I regret?"
—Margaret Carlson, Time, March 20, 2000

For an upper-class white boy, Bush comes on way too hard-ass—at a guess, to make up for being an upper class white boy.
—Molly Ivins, Lou Dubose, "Shrub" (2000)

Beneath the winning optimism of his politics he sometimes shows, even today, a curious air of resentment, which is all the more puzzling for its place in a life so touched by advantage
—Marjorie Williams, The Washington Post, January 7, 2000

The Americans who began choosing our next President tonight took a stand for a leader who unites, and an agenda that inspires. A messenger committed to bringing people together.
—George W. Bush, Iowa Caucus Night, January 24, 2000

Regarding (Bush's) several uses of the f- word, Karen Hughes, Bush's communications director, who travels with him, says, "I don't remember those words being used." She says Bush agrees with those who say such language is inappropriate. Carlson, who says he remembers the words, quotes a Bush aide who says Bush "used to say 'f — k' a lot more before this all started."
—George Will, The Washington Post, August 12, 1999

Is Bush too peevish to be president? Bush's history suggests that he has struggled for much of his life with a kind of defensive anger—an anger more subtle, but perhaps more corrosive, than the temper tantrums of which his rival John McCain has been accused.
—Marjorie Williams, The Washington Post, January 7, 2000

I will return honor and dignity to the White House.
—George W. Bush's, Bob Jones University in South Carolina, February 2, 2000

Bush's macho demeanor in the interview revealed a disturbing lack of restraint, a combination platter of unwelcome traits—stubbornness, as he admits, with side dishes of arrogance and an irritability that couldn't be contained even though things are going well for him.
—Margaret Carlson, Time, March 20, 2000

In a dynasty, you don't have to earn anything. In a democracy, you've got to earn it.
—George W. Bush, New York Times, November 4, 1998

Bush remains the prohibitive favorite to secure the Republican presidential nod, with his oodles of money, legion of supporters and nonpareil political network. Yet he doesn't appear to take the quest seriously.
—Tony Snow, Denver Post, November 14, 1999

"I feel like saying, "God's will be done,' " he said in an interview. "That if I win . . . I know what to do. If I don't win, so be it. So be it."
—George W. Bush, The Washington Post, July 25, 1999

Bush wouldn't have to worry so much about performance if he had a compelling life story to give him gravitas. Unfortunately for him, he's had the least eventful personal history of any major political figure in modern memory.
—Jonathan Alter, Newsweek, November 22, 1999

He failed at business three times, got bailed out by powerful friends, made a fortune at taxpayer expense and became the popular but weak governor of Texas, an evangelical Christian who preaches morality but ducks questions about his own past. And now he might be president?
—Paul Alexander, Rolling Stone, August 5, 1999

"I have always been underestimated," Bush says. "You can understand why. People say, well, he's Daddy's boy and has never done anything of accomplishment. But that's good. I'd rather be underestimated than overestimated."
—U.S. News & World Report, February 21, 2000

The administration I'll bring is a group of men and women who...will see service to our country as a great privilege and who will not stain the house.
--- George W. Bush, Des Moines Register Debate, Iowa, January 15, 2000

Our nation still has determined enemies, who resent our values and hate our successes. The Evil Empire has passed, but evil remains.
—Governor George W. Bush, Remarks at Bob Jones University,
    February 2, 2000